POVERTY BITTERNESS SYNDROME

HOW UNHEALED BITTERNESS TURNS BOLDNESS INTO DESTRUCTION

Poverty Bitterness Syndrome

How Unhealed Bitterness Turns Strength Into Destruction

LEVI SAP NEI THANG

POVERTY BITTERNESS SYNDROME

ISBN: 978-0-9792993-9-1
Library of Congress Control Number: 2026912151

Cover design by Levi Sap Nei Thang.
Published by Levi Sap Nei Thang

Printed in the United States of America.
May 2026.

Preface

Human behavior is rarely as simple as it appears on the surface.

Some people grow gentle through suffering. Others grow guarded, reactive, emotionally hardened, or trapped in patterns of conflict, bitterness, instability, manipulation, or emotional survival. Behaviors that appear irrational, cruel, defensive, controlling, emotionally chaotic, or destructive often develop through environments shaped by fear, instability, deprivation, humiliation, neglect, rejection, emotional insecurity, or prolonged psychological survival.

This book was written to examine what happens when survival never fully heals, not to condemn wounded people.

Many individuals learn emotional patterns during painful environments that later continue long after the original danger has passed. Emotional defensiveness, conflict-seeking, distrust, shame, emotional domination, manipulation, hypervigilance, bitterness, relational instability, and emotional exhaustion are often not random behaviors. They are frequently adaptive responses that once helped a person endure difficult emotional realities.

Poverty can wound the body, but bitterness wounds the heart. A person may escape hardship outwardly yet still carry a survival-war mindset internally — one that slowly turns strength into aggression, relationships into cages, and kindness into fuel for exploitation.

The tragedy is that survival mechanisms which once protected a person can later begin destroying relationships, emotional peace, trust, self-awareness, and even conscience itself when they remain unexamined and unhealed.

Throughout this book, I explore patterns I personally observed, experienced, reflected upon, and tried to understand over many years. Some chapters examine emotional aggression, bitterness, relational collapse, shame, emotional manipulation, and the psychological effects of prolonged survival conditioning. Other chapters focus on healing, discernment, forgiveness, emotional boundaries, gratitude, accountability, and the possibility of emotional restoration without losing kindness or humanity.

This book does not claim that every wounded person becomes destructive. Nor does it suggest that all difficult behavior originates from poverty, hardship, or suffering alone. Human behavior is complex. People respond to pain differently. Some individuals become compassionate through suffering. Others become emotionally hardened. Some heal. Some remain trapped in cycles that repeat across relationships and generations.

At its core, this book asks an important question:

> What happens when emotional survival becomes permanent?

And perhaps even more importantly:

> Can people learn how to heal without becoming emotionally cold, bitter, or destructive themselves?

I believe they can.

Healing may not erase the past, but emotional patterns are not necessarily permanent. Awareness, accountability, emotional honesty, discernment, boundaries, forgiveness, gratitude, and emotionally safe environments can gradually interrupt cycles that once appeared immovable.

The goal of healing is not emotional numbness.

The goal is emotional wisdom.

A healed person is not someone who no longer feels pain. A healed person is someone who learns how to remain human without allowing pain to control who they become.

This book is offered not as a final authority on human behavior but as a reflection on survival, emotional conditioning, relational damage, and the difficult journey toward healing and emotional maturity.

If these pages help even one person recognize destructive cycles, understand emotional wounds more clearly, protect their peace wisely, or heal without losing compassion, then this work has fulfilled its purpose.

Survival may protect a person physically while damaging them emotionally.

But emotional patterns are not necessarily permanent.

Healing becomes possible through awareness, discernment, boundaries, accountability, gratitude, forgiveness, and emotional wisdom.

Dedication

To those who endured more than they should have.

To those who learned to survive before they learned to live.

To those who are still searching for peace in a life they fought hard to build.

TABLE OF CONTENTS

Introduction

Some people appear strong at first encounter.

They move quickly, speak with certainty, and project unwavering confidence. They challenge others without visible fear, dominate conversations, and often present themselves as decisive, fearless, or exceptionally capable. To observers, these traits may initially resemble leadership, resilience, independence, or emotional strength.

Yet over time, something begins to fracture beneath the surface.

Conflict repeatedly follows them. Relationships become strained or unstable. Trust gradually deteriorates. Environments that initially felt energized begin to feel emotionally exhausting, unpredictable, or tense. Cycles of misunderstanding, blame, emotional volatility, defensiveness, manipulation, bitterness, emotional withdrawal, or relational collapse begin emerging with increasing consistency.

What first appeared to be strength may instead reflect something far more complex.

In many cases, these patterns do not originate in adulthood alone. They are often shaped gradually through early emotional experiences, particularly within childhood and the home environment. Repeated exposure to instability, emotional inconsistency, chronic conflict, deprivation, humiliation, excessive criticism, neglect, fear, emotional insecurity, conditional acceptance, or prolonged survival-based environments can profoundly influence the way individuals learn to interpret safety, attachment, trust, control, identity, vulnerability, and emotional survival.

Over time, adaptations that were once protective may become deeply embedded behavioral systems. Responses originally developed to endure difficult environments can later persist long after the original conditions have disappeared. What once functioned as emotional protection may eventually contribute to instability in relationships, communication, accountability, emotional regulation, trust, and self-perception.

This book explores how unresolved survival conditioning can evolve into recurring cycles of emotional and relational dysfunction. It examines bitterness, emotional defensiveness, manipulation, shame, emotional domination, conflict dependency, relational collapse, emotional exhaustion, hypervigilance, emotional desensitization, and the gradual hardening that sometimes occurs when suffering remains unresolved for too long.

At the same time, this book also explores healing.

Not all wounded people remain trapped in destructive cycles permanently. Emotional patterns learned through survival are often deeply rooted, but they are not necessarily irreversible. Healing becomes possible when awareness, accountability, emotional honesty, discernment, boundaries, forgiveness, gratitude, emotional safety, and healthy relational structure gradually interrupt old patterns and create new ones.

You will learn:

- how survival-based behaviors can masquerade as strength
- how childhood experiences and emotional conditioning shape adult relational patterns
- why conflict can become emotionally familiar or psychologically reinforcing
- how shame, bitterness, manipulation, and emotional defensiveness develop over time
- why some individuals normalize cruelty, domination, or emotional instability
- how unresolved pain spreads into relationships and social environments
- why emotionally soft individuals often become vulnerable to manipulation or emotional exhaustion
- how discernment and boundaries protect emotional health
- how healing requires more than physical survival
- how emotional wisdom allows people to remain compassionate without becoming naïve
- how to recognize destructive cycles without becoming emotionally consumed by them
- how healing can occur without losing kindness, humanity, or emotional depth

The purpose of this book is to encourage healing, emotional awareness, accountability, and growth while approaching these patterns with honesty, compassion, and understanding.

Human behavior is complex, and every person carries a history shaped by experiences, environments, relationships, emotional conditioning, and survival strategies. Some people become compassionate through suffering. Others become emotionally hardened. Some heal. Others remain trapped inside patterns that repeat across relationships and generations.

Rather than labeling people simplistically, this work seeks to identify recurring emotional and relational patterns that often remain misunderstood, normalized, or overlooked.

Recognition matters because unresolved patterns rarely disappear on their own.

Left unexamined, they tend to repeat themselves across relationships, families, environments, and stages of life.

But awareness creates possibility.

Once patterns become visible, it becomes possible to respond differently—with greater clarity, emotional wisdom, healthier boundaries, stronger discernment, accountability, and reduced participation in cycles of instability and emotional harm.

Understanding the pattern is the first step toward no longer being controlled by it.

And healing begins when survival no longer defines the entire future of the heart.

Emotional instability is not limited to one gender, culture, or social class. These patterns may develop in both men and women through different combinations of trauma, conditioning, stress, biological influences, and environmental experiences.

PART I

Understanding The Pattern

Chapter 1
Understanding The Syndrome
Why We Mistake Bitterness for Strength

Opening Quote

"Presentation creates impressions. Repetition reveals structure."
— Levi Sap Nei Thang

Opening Reflection

Some people appear strong immediately.

They speak with certainty, move with confidence, and create the impression of emotional clarity and fearlessness. In uncertain environments, these qualities naturally attract attention and admiration.

But appearance and structure are not always the same thing.

What initially feels powerful may later reveal instability beneath the surface. Behaviors that appear bold, decisive, or emotionally intense can sometimes originate not from grounded strength, but from survival conditioning, emotional pressure, or unresolved internal instability.

This chapter explores how perception forms, why emotionally soft-hearted individuals are often drawn toward visible intensity, and how repeated patterns eventually reveal the difference between presentation and genuine stability.

In This Chapter

This chapter examines how confidence, boldness, intensity, and decisiveness are often mistaken for genuine strength. It explores how survival-based behaviors can initially appear attractive, persuasive, or powerful while concealing deeper instability beneath the surface. Readers will learn how perception is shaped, why emotionally soft-hearted individuals are often drawn toward these dynamics, and how repeated patterns eventually reveal the difference between appearance and structural stability.

Chapter Outline

Chapter Overview

First impressions are rarely neutral. They are formed quickly, often before conscious reasoning has time to engage, and they are heavily influenced by visible signals—confidence, decisiveness, intensity, and presence.

In many environments, these signals are interpreted as strength.

A person who speaks with certainty appears capable. A person who acts quickly appears clear. A person who confronts others directly appears fearless. These qualities create a powerful impression, and that impression often becomes the foundation for trust, admiration, and alignment.

But not all boldness reflects stability.

Some forms of boldness are grounded in clarity and internal balance. Others are formed under pressure—adaptations to instability that continue long after the original conditions have changed.

At first, these two forms look identical.
Over time, they produce very different outcomes.

1.1 Understanding Perception

Perception is the process through which individuals interpret experiences, interactions, and environments. It is shaped not only by present reality but also by past experiences, emotional conditioning, and learned expectations. Over time, repeated exposure to instability or hardship can alter perception, causing neutral situations to be interpreted through a lens of survival, threat, or distrust.

1.2 Understanding Survival-Based Identity

A **survival-based identity** develops when long-term hardship, instability, or emotional insecurity becomes deeply integrated into a person's sense of self. In this state, behaviors originally formed for protection continue even after circumstances improve, influencing relationships, emotional responses, and decision-making patterns.

1.3 Understanding Emotional Conditioning

Emotional conditioning refers to the process through which repeated experiences shape emotional reactions over time. When certain environments consistently produce fear, instability, criticism, or stress, individuals may begin to respond automatically to similar situations, even when immediate danger no longer exists.

1.4 The Speed of Misjudgment

Human perception is designed for efficiency, not accuracy.

When we encounter someone new, we do not begin with a full evaluation. We begin with signals. These signals are processed quickly and subconsciously, forming an impression before reasoning has time to catch up.

Confidence is one of the strongest of these signals.

It reduces uncertainty. It suggests competence. It creates the feeling that the person understands something we may not yet fully see.

This is especially powerful in uncertain environments.
When people are unsure, they look for certainty.
When someone provides it, they gain influence immediately.
The problem is that certainty is not the same as clarity.
And confidence is not proof of either.

1.5 Scenario: The First Encounter

Consider a situation where a new individual enters a professional or social environment.

They speak clearly.
They do not hesitate.
They challenge existing ideas without fear.

They position themselves as someone who "sees the truth" that others are missing.

People notice.
Some admire.
Some feel intimidated.
Some feel drawn.
A soft-hearted individual, in particular, may feel relief.
Finally, someone strong.
Someone decisive.
Someone who is not afraid.
That feeling of relief is the beginning of alignment.
Not because the individual has proven stability.

But because they have reduced uncertainty.

1.6 Why Soft-Hearted People Are Drawn In

Soft-hearted individuals are not weak.
They are adaptive in a different way.
They prioritize harmony, empathy, and understanding.
They avoid unnecessary conflict.
They value connection over dominance.

When they encounter someone who appears strong, direct, and unafraid, it feels complementary.

It feels like balance.
Where they hesitate, the other moves.
Where they soften, the other sharpens.
Where they seek peace, the other appears capable of protecting it.
This creates a powerful dynamic.
Not because the match is stable.
But because it feels complete.

1.7 The Illusion Begins

At this stage, the perception is clean.
The individual is seen as strong.
Their boldness is interpreted as courage.
Their intensity is interpreted as conviction.
There is no reason yet to question it.
But something subtle is already happening.
The observer is not evaluating structure.
They are responding to the presentation.
And presentation, when consistent and confident, can be extremely convincing.

1.8 The Investment Phase — Where Trust Is Built

Before instability appears, there is often a phase of strong positive engagement.
This phase is critical.
Because it builds emotional credibility.
The individual may show care, attention, generosity, and presence. They may listen closely, offer support, and create a sense of emotional safety.
This does not feel strategic.
It feels genuine.
The connection deepens.
The observer begins to feel understood, valued, and seen. The boldness that initially attracted them is now reinforced by what appears to be kindness.
This combination is powerful.
Strength plus care feels rare.
And because it feels rare, it feels trustworthy.

1.9 Scenario: Emotional Bonding

Imagine a soft-hearted person who has always been the one giving, supporting, and understanding others.
They meet someone who not only shows strength but also turns that attention toward them.
They listen.
They validate.
They show interest.
For the first time, the soft-hearted individual feels supported.
This is where attachment forms.

1.10 The Shift No One Sees Coming

The change is not immediate.
It is gradual.
The same intensity that created connection begins to create pressure.
The same confidence that felt reassuring begins to feel rigid.
But the observer does not immediately react to this change.
Because they are still anchored to the beginning.
They remember the care.
They remember the attention.
They remember how it felt.
And so they interpret the shift as temporary.

1.11 Internal Dialogue of the Soft-Hearted Observer

At this stage, the internal dialogue often sounds like this:

> "Maybe they're just stressed."
> "This isn't how they usually are."
> "I just need to communicate better."

These thoughts are not irrational.
They are attempts to preserve coherence.
The observer is trying to reconcile two versions of the same person.
The one they first experienced.
And the one they are now encountering.

1.12 Repetition Reveals Structure

Patterns do not become clear through single events.

They become clear through repetition.
The same type of conflict appears again.
The same reaction occurs.
The same escalation unfolds.
Different situation.
Same outcome.
At first, it feels coincidental.
Then it feels confusing.
Eventually, it feels predictable.
And predictability changes perception.

1.13 Scenario: Repeated Conflict

A disagreement begins.
It could be small.
A difference in opinion.
A minor misunderstanding.
But it escalates quickly.
The conversation shifts from the issue to tone.
From tone to intent.
From intent to character.
By the end, the original issue is gone.
Only tension remains.
Later, another disagreement occurs.
And the same pattern repeats.

1.14 The Breaking Point of Perception

At some point, the observer stops asking:

"What happened?"

And begins asking:

"Why does this always happen?"

That question changes everything.
Because it shifts focus from events to structure.

1.15 Redefining Strength

Once the pattern is visible, the definition of strength begins to change.
Strength is no longer about boldness.

It is about stability.
Strength is no longer about intensity.
It is about consistency.
Strength is no longer about dominance.
It is about the ability to maintain clarity without creating chaos.
This redefinition is not immediate.
It develops through experience.

1.16 The Realization

The observer begins to understand:
What looked like strength…
    was not building stability.
    It was maintaining control.
What looked like courage…
    was not grounded in clarity.
    It was driven by pressure.
What looked like leadership…
    was not creating alignment.
    It was creating cycles.

1.17 The Lesson of the Shiny Wrapper

The Shiny Wrapper is powerful because it resembles strength so closely.

It is not always entirely false. It is often incomplete. The visible signals appear convincing because some aspects of strength may genuinely exist. But without stability, accountability, and consistency, the structure eventually begins collapsing under pressure.

It shows the visible signals of strength without revealing the underlying structure.

And without time, that structure cannot be seen.

1.18 Financial Insecurity and Psychological Conditioning

Since Poverty Bitterness Syndrome originates within prolonged conditions of deprivation and financial insecurity, unresolved emotional wounds may later manifest through excessive financial focus, material comparison, resentment toward success, survival-driven decision-making, or unhealthy relationships with money and status.

Because financial insecurity often remains psychologically central within Poverty Bitterness Syndrome, some individuals may become disproportionately focused on relationships that provide access to financial stability, status, influence, opportunity, or upward mobility.

This does not apply to everyone who experiences poverty or hardship. Many individuals develop resilience, gratitude, integrity, and empathy despite severe deprivation.

1.19 Reader Reflection

Think about someone you have admired for their boldness.

Now consider:

> Did their actions create stability over time?
> Or did they create repeated tension?
> Did their presence bring clarity?
> Or did it bring cycles?

Were you responding to who they were…

> Or how they appeared?

Key Insight

Not everything that appears bold, confident, or intense reflects genuine strength. Real strength reveals itself over time through stability, consistency, accountability, and the ability to create clarity rather than chaos.

Summary

This chapter examined how confidence, intensity, boldness, and decisiveness can create the appearance of strength before deeper behavioral patterns become visible. It explored how emotionally soft-hearted individuals may become drawn toward visible certainty, particularly in uncertain environments, and how repeated interaction gradually reveals whether apparent strength is grounded in stability or sustained by pressure, emotional intensity, or instability.

The chapter also explored how external presentation can sometimes conceal unresolved emotional patterns beneath the surface. Over time, however, repeated behaviors tend to expose the underlying structure of a person's emotional stability, accountability, and relational health.

Ultimately, genuine strength was redefined not as dominance, emotional intensity, or outward confidence alone, but as consistency, self-control, accountability, emotional stability, and the ability to create clarity rather than chaos over time.

Conclusion

Not everything that looks strong is stable.
Not everything that feels intense is meaningful.
Not everything that moves quickly is clear.
Clarity comes with time.
Real strength reveals itself through what it builds—not merely through how it appears.

Ending Reflections

First impressions are powerful because human beings naturally respond to visible signals before deeper structure becomes clear. Confidence, boldness, intensity, decisiveness, and emotional certainty can easily create the appearance of strength long before stability has actually been tested over time.

This is why many people become emotionally invested before fully recognizing the deeper patterns underneath the presentation.

What initially feels attractive, reassuring, fearless, or emotionally compelling may eventually reveal cycles of pressure, instability, escalation, defensiveness, or repeated conflict. The shift is often difficult to recognize at first because perception often remains anchored to the early experience of admiration, connection, or emotional certainty.

Over time, however, repeated patterns reveal what presentation alone cannot permanently conceal.

Real strength does not merely attract attention in the beginning. Real strength creates stability over time. It allows relationships, communication, trust, accountability, and emotional safety to remain intact even during pressure, disagreement, or difficulty.

The deeper lesson is not that confidence or boldness are inherently dangerous. Rather, it is that visible intensity should never automatically be mistaken for emotional maturity, structural stability, or genuine strength.

Wisdom develops when perception learns to observe not only presentation, but also patterns, outcomes, consistency, accountability, and long-term emotional impact.

Ending Quotes

"Presentation creates impressions. Repetition reveals structure."
— Levi Sap Nei Thang

"Boldness without stability eventually becomes disruption."
— Levi Sap Nei Thang

"People are often drawn to certainty before they understand its source."
— Levi Sap Nei Thang

"What appears fearless may actually be operating from pressure."
— Levi Sap Nei Thang

"Strength is measured by what remains stable over time."
— Levi Sap Nei Thang

"Some forms of intensity are adaptations to instability, not signs of balance."
— Levi Sap Nei Thang
"Real strength creates clarity, not repeated chaos."
— Levi Sap Nei Thang

"The loudest presence in the room is not always the strongest structure."
— Levi Sap Nei Thang

Review Questions

1. Why are people naturally drawn toward confidence and certainty?
2. How can boldness create the illusion of stability?

3. Why do soft-hearted individuals often feel attracted to emotionally intense personalities?
4. What role does repetition play in revealing deeper patterns?
5. How does genuine strength differ from visible intensity?
6. Why is stability more important than presentation over time?

Chapter 2
Poverty Bitterness Syndrome
When Survival Does Not End

Opening Quote

"A person may leave hardship physically while remaining emotionally organized around survival."
— Levi Sap Nei Thang

In This Chapter

This chapter explores how prolonged hardship and survival-based conditioning can continue influencing behavior long after external circumstances improve. It examines the psychological effects of scarcity, emotional deprivation, instability, and unresolved resentment, showing how survival responses may gradually become deeply embedded behavioral structures. Readers will learn how internal survival systems shape emotional regulation, relationships, trust, control, and long-term relational stability.

Chapter Outline

Chapter Overview

Survival is not a flaw. It is often the reason a person endures circumstances that would otherwise overwhelm them.

In environments shaped by poverty, instability, or emotional hardship, survival requires adaptation. It demands awareness, speed, control, and resilience. These are not optional traits—they are necessary responses to conditions where safety is uncertain, and resources are limited.

But survival is not meant to be permanent.

This chapter examines what happens when survival does not transition—when the patterns that once protected an individual begin to define them.

Poverty Bitterness Syndrome is not about poverty alone. It is about what remains after poverty is no longer present.

It is important to recognize that not every individual who experiences poverty, deprivation, or hardship develops these patterns. Many people endure extremely difficult circumstances while maintaining empathy, accountability, emotional stability, generosity, and healthy relational behavior throughout their lives.

Hardship alone does not automatically produce bitterness, chronic conflict, or survival-based instability. The development of these patterns depends on multiple interacting factors, including emotional conditioning, relational environments, coping mechanisms, support systems, personality structure, unresolved trauma, and long-term behavioral reinforcement.

The framework, therefore, does not pathologize poverty itself, but instead examines how unresolved survival conditioning may influence behavior when emotional adaptation does not evolve alongside changing circumstances.

2.1 The Hidden Continuation

Externally, a person may leave poverty.
They may gain financial stability.
They may enter structured environments.
They may build a life that appears successful.
But internally, something may remain unchanged.
The system that was built for survival continues to operate.
It does not automatically update.
It does not recognize that the environment has changed.
And because of that, it continues to produce responses that were once necessary—but are no longer appropriate.

2.2 Scenario: The External Success, Internal Pressure

Consider an individual who grew up with very little.
They experienced instability.
They learned to rely on themselves.
They worked hard and eventually reached a level of success.
From the outside, they have "made it."
But internally, they do not feel safe.
They feel pressure to maintain everything.
They feel alert even in calm environments.
They react quickly to perceived threats, even when none exist.
Their lives have changed.
Their system has not.

2.3 The Real-World Origins of the Pattern

Survival patterns are not theoretical.

They are formed in real conditions.
There may have been times when food was not guaranteed.
When stability was uncertain.
When the future felt unpredictable.
These are not small experiences.
They shape how the world is understood.
In such environments, a person learns quickly:
Nothing is guaranteed.
Everything can be taken.
You must act quickly before opportunities disappear.
This is not pessimism.
It is an adaptation.

2.4 Family Survival Mode

In many cases, the family itself is in survival mode.
Parents are focused on providing.
Stress is constant.
Emotional expression becomes secondary.
There may not be time for connection.
There may not be space for softness.
Conversations revolve around necessity, not emotion.
As a result, the child learns:

- Survival comes first.
- Feelings come later—or not at all.

2.5 Scenario: Growing Up Without Emotional Space

A child grows up in a household where everything is about making ends meet.
There is no intentional harm.
But there is also no emotional teaching.
No one explains feelings.
No one models vulnerability.
No one demonstrates how to process hurt.
The child learns to function.
But not to process.

2.6 When Emotional Expression Was Forbidden

Many individuals grow up in environments where emotional expression is discouraged, criticized, or treated as weakness. Crying is mocked. Vulnerability is corrected. Emotional openness is interpreted as instability rather than honesty.

Children may hear statements such as:

"Stop crying."
"Be strong."
"Don't be emotional."
"Only weak people cry."

Over time, these repeated messages shape emotional conditioning. The child slowly learns that certain emotions are not permitted to be expressed openly. Sadness becomes shameful. Vulnerability becomes dangerous. Emotional suppression becomes associated with strength and survival.

As a result, some individuals develop an external identity built around hardness, emotional control, or detachment. They may appear strong because they rarely show visible vulnerability. However, emotional suppression is not the same as emotional stability.

Unprocessed emotions do not disappear simply because they are hidden. Suppressed grief, fear, humiliation, disappointment, and emotional pain often remain active beneath the surface. Over time, these unresolved emotions may reappear indirectly through anger, bitterness, emotional numbness, emotional withdrawal, irritability, relational instability, or disproportionate emotional reactions.

In many cases, the individual was never taught how to regulate emotions in a healthy way. They were only taught how to conceal them.

This creates an important distinction:

- Healthy emotional regulation allows a person to experience emotions without becoming controlled by them.
- Emotional suppression attempts to deny or bury emotions entirely.

The two are not the same.

A person who never cries is not automatically emotionally strong. In some cases, they may simply have learned that emotional expression was unsafe. Likewise, individuals who become uncomfortable when others express sadness or vulnerability may unconsciously repeat the emotional rules they themselves were taught during childhood.

Over time, emotional suppression can create relational difficulties. The individual may struggle to communicate emotional needs, avoid vulnerability, disconnect during conflict, or respond defensively when emotional conversations arise. Some individuals become emotionally distant not because they lack feelings, but because they were conditioned to fear emotional exposure itself.

One of the most misunderstood ideas in many environments is the belief that emotional numbness equals strength.

True emotional strength is not the inability to cry.

True emotional strength is the ability to remain emotionally honest while maintaining self-control, wisdom, and stability.

2.7 Understanding Resentment

Resentment is the prolonged emotional carryover of unresolved anger, perceived unfairness, humiliation, or repeated hardship. It develops when painful experiences are not fully processed, but instead remain internalized over time, gradually shaping perception, emotional response, and behavior.

Unlike temporary anger, resentment persists. It can influence how individuals interpret relationships, opportunities, authority, criticism, and social interactions. When left unresolved, resentment may contribute to chronic bitterness, defensiveness, distrust, comparison, and recurring interpersonal conflict.

2.8 Understanding Scarcity Mindset

A **scarcity mindset** is a psychological state shaped by prolonged exposure to limitation, instability, or lack. In this condition, attention becomes narrowly focused on immediate needs, threats, or survival concerns, often making long-term planning, emotional stability, and trust more difficult to maintain.

2.9 Understanding Emotional Deprivation

Emotional deprivation occurs when consistent emotional support, affection, reassurance, or psychological safety is absent during important developmental periods. Over time, this absence may affect self-worth, trust, emotional regulation, and the ability to form stable relationships.

2.10 Understanding Survival Mode

Survival mode is a prolonged psychological and emotional state in which the mind prioritizes protection, urgency, and immediate adaptation over reflection, stability, or long-term emotional processing. Behaviors formed in survival mode may continue long after the original environment has changed.

2.11 Scarcity, Resentment, and Psychological Adaptation

Long-term financial hardship affects more than material conditions.

Over time, it can shape perception, emotional response, and behavioral structure.

When individuals are raised in environments defined by instability, limitation, or repeated deprivation, survival becomes the primary focus. Attention narrows toward immediate needs, immediate threats, and immediate outcomes.

This creates what is often described as a scarcity-oriented mindset.
The future feels uncertain.

Security feels temporary.
Opportunities appear limited or unevenly distributed.

As these experiences accumulate, emotional effects may begin to develop alongside practical ones.

Feelings of resentment, frustration, humiliation, or perceived unfairness can gradually become internalized. Repeated exposure to comparison, exclusion, or lack of opportunity may produce deep sensitivity toward status, recognition, and control.

Over time, the emotional response to hardship may continue even after conditions improve.

The external environment changes.
But the internal system remains organized around survival.

This can affect relationships, trust, emotional regulation, and long-term stability.

Some individuals become highly reactive to perceived disrespect or inequality. Others become emotionally guarded, withdrawn, or chronically defensive.

In many cases, these responses are not deliberate.
They are adaptive behaviors formed under prolonged stress.

Without awareness and repair, however, the same survival mechanisms that once provided protection can later create instability in personal relationships, workplaces, communities, and systems of support.

2.12 Comparison and the Formation of Pressure

At the same time, the individual may observe others who live differently.
They see stability.
They see comfort.
They see what appears to be ease.
This creates comparison.
Not always spoken.
But deeply felt.

> "Why is their life different?"
> "What do they have that I don't?"
> "What do I need to do to get there?"

These questions do not disappear.
They transform into a drive.

2.13 The Drive to Never Go Back

This is one of the most powerful forces in the pattern.
The individual is not only moving forward.
They are running from the past.
They are determined:
Never to be poor again.
Never to feel powerless again.
Never to depend on uncertainty again.
This creates intensity.
And that intensity can look like ambition.
But it is often driven by fear.

2.14 Emotional Carryover

Even when circumstances improve, emotional responses remain.
Trust is still difficult.
Vulnerability still feels unsafe.
Control still feels necessary.
The individual may not consciously think about the past.
But their reactions are shaped by it.

2.15 Internal Dialogue of the Survivor

"I can't relax."
"If I lose this, everything falls apart."
"I have to stay ahead."

These thoughts are not always spoken.
But they guide behavior.

2.16 Unresolved Bitterness

Not all experiences are processed.
Some are carried.
The individual may not openly express resentment.
But it exists beneath the surface.
Toward circumstances.
Toward inequality.
Toward what they lacked.
This bitterness is not always visible.
But it remains active beneath perception.
And because it is not resolved, it continues to shape perception.

2.17 The Absence of Modeled Affection

In survival environments, love may exist—but it is not always expressed in a way that can be learned.
There may be no clear model of:

- How to show affection
- How to receive it
- How to trust it

The individual grows up without a stable reference point.
So later in life, when they encounter connection, it may feel unfamiliar.
Even uncomfortable.

2.18 Scenario: When Love Feels Unfamiliar

Someone shows genuine care.
Patience.
Kindness.
Stability.
Instead of feeling safe, the individual feels uncertain.

> "Why are they like this?"
> "What do they want?"
> "This doesn't feel normal."

Because it is not familiar.

2.19 From Survival to Control

The patterns that once protected the individual begin to change form.
Awareness becomes suspicion.
Strength becomes rigidity.
Self-reliance becomes isolation.
This is not intentional.
It is structural.

2.20 Why It Still Looks Like Strength

From the outside, the individual appears driven.
Focused. Determined. Unafraid.
These qualities are often rewarded.
So the pattern continues.
Because it works—at least initially.

2.21 The Turning Point

Over time, something begins to break.
Relationships become strained.
Conflict becomes frequent.
Stability becomes difficult to maintain.
The same intensity that created success begins to create problems.

2.22 Scenario: Repeating the Same Outcome

The individual enters multiple relationships.

At first, things go well.
But over time, conflict appears.
Different person.
Same pattern.
Eventually, the question arises:

"Why does this keep happening?"

2.23 Recreating the Past

Without realizing it, the individual recreates the environment they escaped.
Not physically.
But emotionally.
Instability returns.
Conflict returns.
Pressure returns.
Because the internal system is still operating from that place.

2.24 The Core Mechanism

This is the essence of Poverty Bitterness Syndrome:

The environment has changed.
The system has not.

And because of that, the past continues to shape the present.

2.25 Biology Is Not Destiny

Emotional instability, unresolved trauma, chronic resentment, and poor emotional regulation can affect both men and women.

Biological factors, stress, hormonal fluctuations, environmental conditioning, trauma exposure, and learned behavioral patterns may all influence emotional responses differently across individuals.

However, biological influence does not remove personal responsibility, accountability, or the capacity for emotional healing, self-control, and behavioral change.

Key Insight

Survival responses that once protected an individual can become long-term behavioral structures when they remain unresolved after circumstances change. The environment may improve while the internal system continues operating from fear, scarcity, and instability.

Summary

This chapter examined how survival-based conditioning can remain psychologically active long after external hardship has ended. It explored how prolonged exposure to instability, scarcity, emotional deprivation, and unresolved stress may gradually shape perception, emotional regulation, trust, control, and relational behavior.

The chapter distinguished poverty itself from the long-term internalization of survival-based emotional structures, emphasizing that hardship alone does not automatically produce bitterness, chronic conflict, or instability. Instead, the continuation of these patterns depends on unresolved emotional conditioning, coping mechanisms, and repeated behavioral reinforcement over time.

The chapter also explored how fear of returning to hardship can create ongoing pressure, emotional guardedness, hypervigilance, resentment, and difficulty experiencing stability or vulnerability as safe. Even when external conditions improve, the internal system may continue operating from survival.

Ultimately, the chapter demonstrated that the central issue is not the existence of hardship itself, but the continuation of survival-based adaptation after the environment has changed. Without awareness, reflection, and emotional repair, protective behaviors formed under pressure may gradually become long-term structures that recreate instability within adult relationships, communication, and personal identity.

Conclusion

Survival is powerful.
It allows human beings to endure conditions that would otherwise overwhelm them. It creates resilience, adaptation, awareness, and persistence under pressure.

But survival is not meant to become a permanent emotional identity.

When survival continues long after the environment has changed, protective behaviors can gradually become limiting structures. Fear replaces trust. Vigilance replaces peace. Control replaces connection. The individual may continue progressing externally while remaining internally organized around instability, scarcity, and emotional pressure.

The tragedy is not that survival once existed.
The tragedy is when the mind never learns that survival is no longer necessary.

Healing begins when the individual recognizes that stability, safety, emotional regulation, and connection are not threats to survival, but signs that survival no longer has to govern the present.

Ending Reflections

Survival is one of the most powerful adaptive systems within human behavior.

In conditions of poverty, instability, emotional deprivation, or prolonged uncertainty, survival responses are often necessary for endurance, protection, and continuation. These adaptations are not signs of weakness. They are evidence of the human capacity to persist under pressure.

The difficulty emerges when survival does not evolve after circumstances change.

A person may leave environments of hardship physically while remaining emotionally organized around scarcity, urgency, distrust, control, defensiveness, or fear of loss. Even when external conditions improve, the internal system may continue operating as though danger is still present. As a result, behaviors once necessary for protection may gradually become sources of instability in relationships, communication, emotional regulation, and long-term personal well-being.

Poverty Bitterness Syndrome is therefore not about material poverty alone. It is about unresolved survival conditioning that continues shaping perception, emotional response, and behavior long after the original environment has changed.

Not every individual who experiences hardship develops these patterns. Many people endure severe adversity while maintaining empathy, accountability, emotional warmth, generosity, and relational stability throughout their lives. The issue is not poverty itself, but the long-term internalization of survival-based emotional structures that remain unexamined and unresolved.

Over time, survival-based thinking can quietly reshape identity. Fear becomes vigilance. Self-protection becomes control. Emotional guardedness becomes isolation. The individual may continue moving forward externally while remaining psychologically trapped in the emotional logic of the past.

Real healing begins when survival no longer controls perception. Stability develops when the individual learns that safety, trust, vulnerability, emotional regulation, and connection are no longer threats to survival, but necessary foundations for long-term emotional health.

Ending Quotes

"Survival protects the individual. Permanence traps them inside the adaptation."
— Levi Sap Nei Thang

"A person can escape hardship physically while remaining emotionally governed by it."
— Levi Sap Nei Thang

"Fear of returning to the past can quietly dominate the present."
— Levi Sap Nei Thang

"Scarcity may disappear externally while continuing internally."
— Levi Sap Nei Thang

"Unresolved survival conditioning often continues long after the danger has passed."
— Levi Sap Nei Thang

"Not every survival behavior remains healthy once survival is no longer necessary."
— Levi Sap Nei Thang

"The body may leave hardship before the nervous system recognizes safety."
— Levi Sap Nei Thang

"Some people continue fighting battles that no longer exist because the internal system never learned that the environment changed."
— Levi Sap Nei Thang

Review Questions

1. How can survival-based conditioning continue influencing behavior after external circumstances improve?
2. What is the difference between temporary hardship and long-term survival-based identity formation?
3. How does a scarcity mindset affect emotional regulation, trust, and long-term stability?
4. Why is it important to distinguish poverty itself from unresolved survival conditioning?
5. How can emotional deprivation during childhood affect adult relationships and attachment patterns?
6. Why may individuals who grew up in instability struggle to feel safe even in stable environments?
7. How can fear of returning to hardship shape ambition, control, or emotional intensity?
8. In what ways can unresolved resentment continue influencing perception and behavior over time?
9. Why can healthy affection, patience, or stability sometimes feel unfamiliar or uncomfortable to individuals shaped by survival environments?
10. What does it mean when "the environment has changed, but the system has not"?

Chapter 3
The Need for Opposition
When Identity Requires an Enemy

Opening Quote

"When conflict becomes familiar enough, peace can begin to feel like emptiness."
— *Levi Sap Nei Thang*

In This Chapter

This chapter examines how unresolved survival conditioning can transform conflict from a temporary disagreement into a recurring psychological structure. It explores why opposition becomes emotionally organizing, how escalation patterns develop, and how repeated conflict reshapes relationships, communication, accountability, and systems of stability. Readers will also learn how chronic conflict gradually expands from isolated interactions into broader relational and social environments.

Chapter Outline

Chapter Overview

Conflict is not always about disagreement.

In stable systems, conflict arises when something needs to be addressed. It has a beginning, a middle, and—most importantly—an end.

But in certain patterns, conflict does not resolve.
It repeats.
It expands.
And over time, it becomes part of identity.

This chapter examines how survival-based patterns extend outward into behavior—how conflict becomes necessary, how opposition is created, and why resolution becomes increasingly difficult.

Many maladaptive emotional and relational patterns do not emerge suddenly in adulthood but are gradually formed during childhood through repeated experiences within the home environment. Early family dynamics, emotional conditioning, instability, neglect, excessive control, or chronic conflict can shape the psychological frameworks through which individuals later interpret relationships, attachment, responsibility, and emotional safety. Over time, these patterns may become deeply internalized and continue influencing adult behavior unless consciously recognized and addressed.

3.1 Conflict as Structure

For most people, conflict is situational.
It is tied to specific events. Once those events are resolved, the conflict fades.
But for someone operating from a survival-based system, conflict can serve a different role.
It provides structure.
Without conflict, there may be uncertainty.
Without opposition, there may be no clear direction.
Conflict creates clarity.
It defines sides.
It creates movement.
It gives purpose.
This is why it can become necessary.

3.2 Scenario: Calm Feels Unfamiliar

An individual enters a stable environment.
There is no tension.
No urgency.
No immediate problem to solve.
At first, this feels positive.
But over time, something shifts.
They begin to feel restless.
Uncertain.
Even uncomfortable.
Because calm is not what they are used to.
Conflict, on the other hand, feels familiar.

3.3 The Search for Friction

When conflict becomes part of the internal structure, the individual may begin to look for it.
Not consciously.
But through interpretation.
A neutral comment may feel like criticism.
A difference of opinion may feel like opposition.
A delay may feel like disrespect.
These interpretations create friction.
And friction becomes the starting point for conflict.

3.4 Understanding Escalation

Escalation is the process through which conflict, tension, or emotional intensity increases beyond the original issue. Rather than moving toward resolution, interactions expand in intensity, emotional charge, or relational impact.

3.5 Understanding Opposition

Opposition is the perception or framing of disagreement, boundaries, or difference as personal resistance or hostility. Over time, repeated opposition-based interpretation may create division, defensiveness, and recurring conflict.

3.6 Understanding Conflict Structure

A **conflict structure** develops when conflict becomes psychologically organizing rather than situational. In this state, tension, opposition, and emotional intensity provide direction, identity, or familiarity, making calm or stability feel uncomfortable or unfamiliar.

3.7 Understanding Accountability

Accountability is the willingness to acknowledge actions, recognize impact, and accept responsibility for behavior without deflection or justification. Accountability is essential for repair, trust, and long-term relational stability.

3.8 Behavioral Pattern Profile

The pattern described in this chapter is not defined by a single action, but by consistent repetition over time. While individual situations may vary, the underlying behaviors tend to follow a recognizable structure.

One of the most visible characteristics is the tendency to escalate rather than resolve. Situations that begin as minor disagreements often expand beyond their original scope. The focus shifts away from addressing the issue and toward intensifying the interaction, creating conflict that continues rather than concludes.

This pattern is often reinforced by the misinterpretation of neutral situations. Feedback, differences in perspective, or ordinary delays may be perceived as criticism, opposition, or disrespect. These interpretations generate friction where none was intended, setting the stage for further escalation.

Over time, disagreement is no longer processed as a difference of opinion but as opposition. Interactions become framed in terms of alignment—who is "for" and who is "against." This shift introduces division into environments that would otherwise remain stable.

Another defining feature is the avoidance of accountability. Direct acknowledgment of behavior becomes limited or conditional, often replaced by justification or redirection. The focus moves away from what occurred and toward how others responded, preventing a clear evaluation of the original action.

Because accountability is not fully established, repair does not take place. Without acknowledgment, adjustment, and follow-through, the same pattern repeats. This repetition gradually weakens trust and prevents relationships from stabilizing.

3.9 Distortion and Control in Interaction

In some cases, the pattern extends beyond conflict into how interactions are shaped and influenced.

Communication may become directional rather than reciprocal.
Information may be selectively emphasized or reframed to support a position.
Attention may be guided toward specific interpretations while minimizing others.

This does not always appear overt.

It can present as confidence, certainty, or strong persuasion.
However, over time, the effect becomes noticeable.
Conversations begin to feel unbalanced.
Outcomes repeatedly shift in one direction.

Others may find themselves adjusting, explaining, or defending more than expected.

The dynamic is not defined by a single moment, but by repeated influence over interaction.

3.10 Language as a Tool of Escalation

In many cases, language becomes a primary mechanism through which the pattern operates.

Interaction may shift from communication to control.

Words are no longer used primarily to exchange information, but to direct, pressure, or shape the interaction.

This can take multiple forms.
Statements may become intensified beyond the situation.
Tone may shift to create urgency, dominance, or confrontation.
Language may be used to provoke a reaction rather than encourage resolution.

Over time, the effect becomes cumulative.
Conversations feel less like dialogue and more like positioning.
Responses become defensive rather than collaborative.
Clarity is replaced by tension.
This does not always appear as overt hostility.
It can present as sharpness, insistence, or a persistent challenge.

However, when repeated, the outcome is similar.
Communication becomes strained.
Understanding becomes secondary.
Escalation becomes more likely than resolution.
The pattern is not defined by a single statement.

It is defined by how consistently language is used to increase intensity rather than reduce it.

3.11 The Accumulation of Harm

When these patterns continue without interruption, their impact becomes cumulative.

Strain develops in relationships.
Trust becomes inconsistent.
Communication becomes guarded.
The effect is not always immediate.

But over time, the pattern produces outcomes that are experienced as harmful—both at the individual level and within larger systems such as teams and organizations.

This harm is not always intentional.
But it is consistent.
And consistency determines impact.

Boundaries, when introduced, are frequently misinterpreted. Instead of being understood as limits, they may be perceived as control, rejection, or hostility. This reframing makes it difficult for stable interaction to continue, as the necessary structure is resisted rather than integrated.

Supportive relationships may also become unstable over time. Individuals who initially provide help, opportunity, or consistency can later be reframed as obstacles, particularly when they introduce expectations or limits. This shift creates confusion and redirects conflict toward those who were previously aligned.

At a deeper level, the pattern often depends on conflict itself. In the absence of tension, there may be discomfort or restlessness. Conflict provides structure, direction, and a sense of control, making it difficult to sustain calm environments without disruption.

Narrative also plays a significant role. Situations are frequently reframed in ways that shift attention away from behavior and toward perceived treatment. The discussion moves from what occurred to how the individual feels they were treated, altering the focus of the interaction.

As these behaviors repeat, conflict expands. It moves beyond individual interactions to affect multiple relationships, teams, and environments. What begins as a single issue gradually becomes a broader pattern of instability.

Attention further reinforces the cycle. Conflict draws engagement—whether supportive or oppositional—and this attention can sustain the behavior, allowing it to continue even when it produces negative outcomes.

Over time, the cumulative effect becomes clear. Relationships weaken, collaboration becomes difficult, and structures that once provided stability begin to erode. The pattern does not produce immediate collapse, but gradual instability.

These behaviors are not always intentional, and they do not define a person in isolation. However, when they repeat without interruption or repair, they form a consistent structure. It is this consistency—not the intensity of any single moment—that defines the pattern.

3.12 The Creation of an Opponent

Conflict requires two sides.
When none exist clearly, they may be created.
This does not require intention.
It happens through perception.

Someone who disagrees becomes "against."
Someone who sets a boundary becomes "hostile."
Someone who remains neutral becomes "unsupportive."

Over time, the environment begins to feel divided.
Even when it is not.

3.13 Scenario: The Misinterpreted Interaction

A colleague offers feedback.
It is neutral—even constructive.
But it is received as criticism.
The response escalates.
The conversation shifts.
What could have been resolved quickly becomes something larger.
Later, the same pattern occurs with a different person.
Then again.
Different situation.
Same interpretation.

3.14 Why Kindness Fails to De-escalate

In stable systems, kindness reduces conflict.
In this pattern, it may not.

When someone responds with patience, forgiveness, or restraint, it can be interpreted as weakness—or as confirmation that the behavior is acceptable.

Instead of reducing intensity, it can increase it.

3.15 The Breakdown of Repair

In stable relationships, conflict is followed by repair.
There is acknowledgment.
There is reflection.
There is some form of apology or accountability.
This is what allows relationships, teams, and systems to continue.
In this pattern, that process is often disrupted.

When conflict occurs, the response does not move toward resolution. It moves toward continuation. The focus shifts away from what was done and toward how the situation is interpreted.

As a result, genuine acknowledgment becomes rare.

Apology, when it appears, may be conditional, deflected, or quickly replaced by justification. The underlying behavior remains unchanged, and the cycle continues.

Over time, this creates strain.

Without repair, tension accumulates. Without acknowledgment, trust weakens. Without responsibility, the same conflict repeats in different forms.

3.16 Turning Against Support

One of the more difficult aspects of this pattern is its effect on supportive relationships.

Individuals who offer patience, understanding, or opportunity may initially be received positively. But as patterns continue, those same individuals can become targets of frustration or opposition.

This shift can be confusing.

The very people who provided support, access, or stability may be reframed as obstacles. Their boundaries may be interpreted as betrayal. Their restraint may be seen as a weakness.

Over time, the pattern not only creates conflict.

It redirects it—often toward those who were closest or most supportive.

3.17 Normalization of Support

One of the more difficult aspects of this pattern is the gradual normalization of support.

Opportunities, assistance, patience, or protection that may once have been viewed as meaningful can slowly become interpreted as expected or deserved.

As this shift occurs, appreciation decreases.
Support is no longer experienced as something voluntarily given.
It becomes integrated into expectation.

Over time, acknowledgment may become limited. Gratitude may weaken. The focus shifts away from what has been provided and toward what is still perceived as lacking, unfair, or insufficient.

This creates a difficult dynamic within relationships and systems built on trust or reciprocity.

Individuals who continue offering support may eventually experience increasing strain rather than increasing stability.

3.18 Redirection Toward the Supporter

In some cases, unresolved frustration, instability, or internal conflict may eventually become redirected toward the very individuals who provided support.

This shift can appear contradictory.

The same person who once offered opportunity, patience, guidance, or protection may later become the focus of resentment, opposition, or blame.

This is not always intentional.

But when accountability and reflection remain limited, unresolved tension often seeks direction.

Over time, the relationship changes.
Support becomes strained.
Trust weakens.

The source of stability becomes redefined as part of the conflict itself.

As a result, the pattern not only damages external relationships. It can also damage the very structures and individuals that once helped sustain it.

3.19 The Erosion of the Platform

Support systems—whether relationships, teams, or opportunities—require stability to function.

When patterns of escalation continue without repair, those systems begin to weaken.

At first, the individual may continue to benefit from the structure around them. They may gain visibility, opportunity, or influence.

But without consistent alignment, the same intensity that once created momentum begins to create instability.

Relationships strain.
Trust declines.
Opportunities narrow.

Eventually, the very platform that elevated the individual may begin to erode—not only because of external pressure, but because of repeated internal conflict.

3.20 The Impact Beyond the Individual

The effects of this pattern do not remain contained.
What begins at the individual level gradually extends outward.

At first, the impact appears within individual interactions—misunderstandings, repeated conflict, and strain in close relationships. But over time, the pattern extends beyond the personal level.

Teams begin to feel the disruption.
Organizations experience instability.
Communities become divided.

What appears as isolated conflict gradually becomes systemic tension.

This is not because of a single event.
It is the result of repeated patterns operating without repair.

When escalation replaces resolution, and reaction replaces reflection, the environment begins to adjust around it. Communication becomes cautious. Trust becomes limited. Alignment becomes difficult to maintain.

Over time, the cost increases.
Relationships weaken.
Collaboration breaks down.
Structures that once functioned effectively begin to lose stability.

The pattern not only affects individuals.
It affects the systems they are part of.

3.21 When Strength Becomes Disruption

In earlier stages, the same behaviors may have been interpreted as strength—directness, intensity, confidence, and willingness to confront.

But without stability and repair, these qualities begin to change in their effect.

What once appeared decisive becomes destabilizing.
What once appeared bold becomes disruptive.
What once attracted others begins to push them away.
The shift is not always immediate.

But over time, the outcome becomes clear.
The pattern does not build.
It erodes.

3.22 Internal Dialogue of the Pattern

> "They didn't respond—they're weak."
> "They're trying to control me."
> "I'm right."

These interpretations reinforce behavior.
They remove the need for reflection.

3.23 Response and Role Reversal

When someone does respond, the dynamic shifts again.
Instead of resolution, the response becomes the issue.

The focus moves from:

"What happened?"

to:

"Why are you reacting like this?"

The original behavior disappears from the center.
The reaction replaces it.

3.24 The Expansion Pattern

Conflict does not stay contained.
It grows.
One disagreement becomes multiple.
One person becomes several.
One issue becomes a pattern.
Over time, the individual is not just in conflict.
They are surrounded by it.

3.25 Scenario: Conflict Spreading Across Relationships

An issue begins with one person.
It escalates.
Others become involved.
Sides begin to form.
The situation expands beyond the original interaction.
Eventually, it affects the entire environment.

3.26 The Role of Attention

Conflict attracts attention.
Strong positions.
Clear opposition.
Emotional intensity.
People watch.
Some support.
Some oppose.
Some engage.
Attention reinforces the pattern.
It gives it energy.

3.27 The Attraction to Power

In some cases, the individual seeks proximity to powerful figures.
Not only for support—but for amplification.
Association with power provides:
Visibility
Credibility
Protection
But it also introduces new dynamics.

3.28 Pursuit of Influence and Position

In some cases, the pattern extends into the pursuit of influence.

Positions that offer visibility, authority, or control over direction may be especially appealing—not only for opportunity, but for the structure they provide.

Influence allows the individual to shape interaction, define narratives, and set the terms of engagement.

This does not always appear overt.
It may be framed as ambition, leadership, or a desire for impact.

However, when the underlying pattern remains unchanged, the same dynamics begin to appear at higher levels.

Decisions may become more directional than collaborative.
Dissent may be reframed as opposition.
Control may be prioritized over alignment.
The path toward greater influence can also reflect this pattern.

Advancement may be pursued through intensity, persistent positioning, or alignment with existing power structures. These approaches can be effective in the short term, particularly in environments where visibility and decisiveness are rewarded.

But without stability and accountability, the same pattern that enabled advancement can later introduce instability.

At higher levels, the impact expands.
The behavior does not remain contained within individual interactions.
It begins to affect broader systems—teams, organizations, and communities.

3.29 Scenario: Using Influence as Shield

An individual gains access to a respected figure.
They reference this connection in conflicts.
Others hesitate to challenge them.
This reinforces behavior.
But over time, the same pattern begins to affect that relationship as well.

3.30 Division of Groups

Conflict divides.
It creates sides.
People are no longer responding to the issue.
They are responding to alignment.
Support becomes identity.
Opposition becomes identity.
The environment fragments.

3.31 The Breakdown of Team Dynamics

In collaborative settings, this pattern is especially disruptive.
Teams require trust.
They require flexibility.
They require shared direction.
Conflict-based structure undermines all three.
Over time, the team stops functioning as a unit.

3.32 Scenario: Team Collapse

A team begins with shared goals.
Conflict emerges.
It escalates.
People begin to choose sides.
Communication breaks down.
Eventually, the team no longer functions effectively.

3.33 Why the Pattern Feels Justified

From the inside, everything feels correct.
Each reaction feels justified.

Each escalation feels necessary.
Because it is consistent with the internal system.

3.34 Predictability Over Time

Eventually, the pattern becomes predictable.
A situation begins.
It escalates.
It shifts.
It continues.
Different details.
Same structure.

Key Insight

When conflict becomes psychologically organizing, disagreement is no longer temporary. Opposition begins to provide identity, direction, and emotional structure, making stability feel unfamiliar and resolution difficult to sustain.

Summary

This chapter examined how unresolved survival-based conditioning can transform conflict from a temporary disagreement into a recurring psychological and relational structure. It explored how escalation, opposition, defensiveness, and repeated tension may gradually become emotionally organizing, making stability and calm feel unfamiliar or uncomfortable.

The chapter explained how conflict-based patterns extend beyond isolated interactions and begin affecting communication, accountability, relationships, teams, organizations, and broader systems of stability. It examined how neutral situations may become interpreted as criticism or opposition, how escalation replaces repair, and how repeated conflict gradually weakens trust, collaboration, and emotional safety.

The chapter also explored how language, attention, influence, and narrative positioning can unintentionally reinforce instability over time. Individuals who initially appeared strong, decisive, or influential may gradually create disruption when intensity is not balanced by accountability, reflection, and relational stability.

Ultimately, the chapter demonstrated that recurring conflict is often maintained not by individual events alone, but by repeated structural patterns that continue operating without interruption or repair. When opposition becomes psychologically organizing, conflict no longer functions as a temporary issue to resolve—it becomes part of identity, direction, and emotional familiarity.

Conclusion

Conflict is not always sustained by disagreement alone.

In some patterns, conflict becomes psychologically organizing. It provides direction, identity, emotional activation, and familiarity. Over time, opposition itself begins to create structure.

When this occurs, resolution becomes increasingly difficult—not because solutions are unavailable, but because stability no longer feels emotionally familiar. Escalation replaces reflection. Reaction replaces accountability. Conflict continues not because it is effective, but because it has become integrated into the internal system itself.

Without interruption, repair, and self-awareness, the pattern gradually expands outward—affecting relationships, teams, organizations, and larger systems of stability.

Ending Reflections

Conflict is a natural part of human interaction. In healthy systems, disagreement can lead to clarification, adjustment, accountability, and growth. Conflict becomes harmful not because it exists, but because it stops resolving.

When survival-based conditioning remains psychologically active, conflict may gradually shift from a temporary event into an organizing structure. Opposition begins providing direction. Escalation creates emotional activation. Tension becomes familiar. Over time, calm environments may no longer feel stable, but empty, uncertain, or emotionally uncomfortable.

As this pattern develops, interactions become increasingly shaped by interpretation rather than reality. Neutral situations may be experienced as criticism, boundaries as hostility, and disagreement as personal opposition. Because accountability becomes difficult to sustain, repair weakens. Without repair, the same cycles repeat across relationships, workplaces, teams, and larger social environments.

The effects rarely remain isolated. Repeated escalation gradually reshapes communication, trust, collaboration, and emotional safety. Individuals who initially provided support, opportunity, or stability may eventually become incorporated into the conflict itself. What once created connection begins creating division.

The danger of conflict-based identity is not only relational instability. It is the gradual normalization of escalation as a way of functioning. When opposition becomes emotionally organizing, peace may begin to feel unfamiliar, and resolution may feel emotionally unsatisfying.

Real stability develops when individuals learn that identity does not require enemies, tension, or continuous opposition in order to feel meaningful, directed, or emotionally secure.

Ending Quotes

"When conflict becomes identity, peace begins to feel unfamiliar."
— Levi Sap Nei Thang

"Escalation repeated long enough becomes structure."
— Levi Sap Nei Thang

"Some conflicts continue not because they cannot be solved, but because they have become emotionally organizing."
— Levi Sap Nei Thang

"Without accountability, conflict does not resolve. It multiplies."
— Levi Sap Nei Thang

"Opposition can provide direction when identity lacks stability."
— Levi Sap Nei Thang

"Repeated escalation gradually transforms relationships into systems of tension."
— Levi Sap Nei Thang

Review Questions

1. How can conflict shift from a temporary disagreement into a psychological structure?
2. Why may calm or stability feel uncomfortable to individuals organized around conflict-based patterns?
3. What role does escalation play in maintaining recurring conflict cycles?
4. How can neutral situations become misinterpreted as criticism, opposition, or disrespect?
5. Why is accountability essential for repair and long-term relational stability?
6. How does repeated conflict gradually affect relationships, teams, and larger systems?
7. In what ways can language be used to increase tension rather than encourage resolution?
8. Why do supportive relationships sometimes become targets of frustration or opposition within recurring conflict patterns?
9. How can attention and emotional engagement unintentionally reinforce escalation?
10. What is the difference between strength that creates stability and intensity that creates disruption?

Chapter 4
The Victim-Villain Flip
How Accountability Is Rewritten

Opening Quote

"The most difficult patterns to confront are often the ones that protect themselves through reinterpretation."
— Levi Sap Nei Thang

In This Chapter

This chapter explores how accountability becomes redirected through narrative shifts, emotional reframing, and role reversal. It examines how behavioral focus can move away from the original issue and toward interpretation, perceived mistreatment, or emotional reaction. Readers will learn how deflection protects recurring patterns, why clarity becomes increasingly difficult during escalation, and how unresolved conflict restructures communication and perception.

Chapter Outline

Chapter Overview

Behavior alone does not sustain a pattern.
Interpretation does.

When actions begin creating tension, consequences, resistance, or relational instability, a critical moment appears. In healthy systems, this moment often leads toward reflection, accountability, adjustment, and repair. Conflict may still occur, but clarity remains connected to behavior and responsibility.

In unresolved structural patterns, however, the process frequently shifts in a different direction.

Instead of examining the original issue directly, attention gradually moves toward interpretation, emotional framing, perceived mistreatment, or reaction. Accountability becomes increasingly difficult because acknowledging behavior threatens the stability of the pattern itself. As a result, narratives begin reshaping how events, intentions, boundaries, and interactions are understood.

This chapter examines how accountability becomes redirected through narrative control, deflection, emotional amplification, and role reversal. It explores how the focus of conflict can shift away from actions and toward interpretation, why emotional narratives often become persuasive, and how recurring patterns protect themselves from interruption.

Over time, these shifts affect more than individual disagreements. Communication becomes unstable, clarity weakens, and relationships gradually lose the ability to repair conflict effectively. What began as a single unresolved interaction can eventually develop into a larger system of confusion, defensiveness, and repeated relational instability.

4.1 Understanding Narrative Control

Narrative control refers to attempts to shape how situations, conflicts, or interactions are interpreted by others. This may involve emphasizing certain details, minimizing others, or redirecting focus in ways that influence perception.

4.2 Understanding Deflection

Deflection is the redirection of attention away from the original issue, behavior, or responsibility. Instead of addressing the central concern, focus shifts toward secondary reactions, unrelated details, or the responses of others.

4.3 Understanding Role Reversal

Role reversal occurs when the focus of a conflict shifts from the original behavior to the reaction it produced. In this process, accountability becomes blurred as the responder gradually becomes positioned as the primary problem.

4.4 Understanding Psychological Protection

Psychological protection refers to mental or emotional mechanisms used to avoid discomfort, shame, vulnerability, or perceived threat. While protective responses may reduce immediate emotional distress, they can also prevent reflection, accountability, and long-term healing when overused.

4.5 The Moment of Interruption

Every pattern eventually encounters resistance.
Someone questions it.
Someone sets a boundary.
Someone refuses to continue the cycle.
This moment is critical.
Because it introduces the possibility of change.
But it also introduces discomfort.

4.6 Scenario: The First Challenge

An individual repeats a pattern of escalation.
This time, the other person responds calmly but directly.
They point out the behavior.
They do not attack.
They do not escalate.
They simply name what is happening.
This is a moment of clarity.
But clarity does not always lead to change.

4.7 From Behavior to Interpretation

At this point, the focus can shift.
Instead of examining the behavior, the individual begins to examine the challenge itself.

> "What does this mean?"
> "Why are they saying this?"
> "What are they really trying to do?"

The conversation moves.
Away from action.
Toward interpretation.

4.8 The First Shift

The original issue begins to lose clarity.
Instead of:

> "You did this."

The conversation becomes:

> "You are treating me like this."

This is a subtle but powerful shift.
Because it changes the frame.

4.9 Scenario: A Simple Boundary Becomes a Problem

A person says:

> "I'm not comfortable continuing this conversation if it escalates."

This is a boundary.
But it may be received differently.

"You're shutting me down."
"You don't want to hear me."
"You're controlling the conversation."

The boundary becomes the issue.

4.10 Reassigning Roles

This is where the Victim–Villain Flip begins.
The individual who raised the concern is no longer the one seeking clarity.
They become the source of the problem.
The one being questioned becomes the one being treated unfairly.
Roles shift.
Not through denial.
But through reinterpretation.

4.11 Internal Dialogue of the Flip

"They're attacking me."
"They don't understand me."
"They're trying to control me."

These interpretations feel real.
Because they align with the internal system.

4.12 Emotional Amplification

Emotion strengthens narrative.
When a situation is framed in terms of harm or unfairness, it becomes more compelling—not only to the individual, but to observers.
Emotion adds weight.
It adds urgency.
It shifts attention.

4.13 Scenario: The Escalated Narrative

A disagreement occurs.
It is small.
But it becomes framed as:

"This always happens."
"They always treat me this way."

"This is not okay."

The situation expands.
Past experiences are brought in.
The present becomes part of a larger story.

4.14 The Use of Past Experience

Past hardship is real.
It shapes perception.
But in this pattern, it can also be used to reinterpret the present.

"What I went through…"

"What people have done to me…"

These statements are not false.
But they shift the focus.
From current behavior.
To the historical context.

4.15 Why It Feels Convincing

The narrative works because it is not entirely fabricated.
It contains truth.
It contains emotion.
It contains coherence.
But it is incomplete.
It does not fully represent the current situation.

4.16 The Displacement of Responsibility

Responsibility does not disappear.
It moves.
Instead of:

"What did I do?"

The focus becomes:

"How was I treated?"

This changes the conversation.
It removes the need for behavioral evaluation.

4.17 Scenario: Conversation Breakdown

One person tries to return to the original issue.
"But we're talking about what happened earlier…"
The response shifts again.

"You're not listening."
"You're dismissing me."

The conversation cannot return.
Because the frame has changed.

4.18 The Experience of the Other Person

For the person trying to resolve the issue, this is disorienting.
They begin with clarity.
They end with confusion.
They may start questioning themselves.

"Did I say it wrong?"
"Am I being unfair?"
"Did I miss something?"

This is how the pattern pulls them in.

4.19 Expansion Beyond the Moment

The narrative does not stay contained.
It spreads.
It may be shared with others.
Retold.
Reinforced.
Each time, it becomes more stable.

4.20 Scenario: External Reinforcement

The individual shares their version with others.
Those who hear it respond emotionally.
They support.
They validate.
They do not see the full picture.
But they respond to the narrative.
This strengthens it.

4.21 Protection of the Pattern

This reversal pattern is not random.
It serves a protective function within the interaction.
It protects the pattern.
It prevents interruption.
It allows continuation.

4.22 Escalation Under Pressure

When challenged again, the narrative may escalate.
The claims may become stronger.
More serious.
More difficult to ignore.
This increases pressure.
It forces engagement.

4.23 The Stability of the New Narrative

Over time, the new narrative becomes the reference point.
Not the original event.
Not the behavior.
But the interpretation.
Everything is filtered through it.

4.24 Predictability of the Flip

Like other patterns, this becomes predictable.
A challenge appears.
The narrative shifts.
Roles change.
The original issue disappears.

4.25 The Cost of the Flip

Clarity is lost.
Resolution becomes difficult.
Trust weakens.
Over time, communication breaks down.
Not because people stop talking.
But because they are no longer talking about the same thing.

Key Insight

Patterns are often protected not through direct denial, but through reinterpretation. When accountability is redirected toward perceived mistreatment, clarity weakens and recurring conflict becomes increasingly difficult to interrupt.

Summary

This chapter examined how recurring behavioral patterns often protect themselves through reinterpretation, emotional reframing, deflection, and role reversal. It explored how accountability can gradually become displaced as conversations shift away from behavior and toward perception, reaction, emotional positioning, or perceived mistreatment.

The chapter explained how narrative control influences interpretation by emphasizing certain details, minimizing others, and reshaping how conflicts are understood. It also examined how emotionally compelling narratives may feel convincing because they frequently contain elements of truth, personal pain, or genuine emotional experience, even when they do not fully represent the original issue.

Over time, these shifts weaken clarity within communication. The original behavior becomes increasingly difficult to evaluate because the interaction is no longer centered on accountability alone. Instead, attention moves toward defending intention, responding to emotional framing, or managing escalating reinterpretation.

The chapter also explored the psychological impact on others within the interaction, including confusion, self-doubt, emotional exhaustion, and difficulty maintaining clarity or stable resolution. As these patterns repeat, relationships weaken not only because of conflict itself, but because communication gradually loses the ability to remain anchored to behavior and responsibility.

Ultimately, the chapter demonstrated that unresolved patterns are often sustained not through direct denial alone, but through narrative structures that protect the pattern from interruption. When reinterpretation replaces accountability, recurring conflict becomes increasingly difficult to resolve or repair.

Conclusion

Not all misunderstandings are accidental.

Some emerge from patterns that reorganize conflict through interpretation, emotional reframing, and role reversal.

When behavior is no longer the center of evaluation, clarity begins to weaken. Conversations shift away from accountability and toward perception, intention, reaction, and emotional positioning. Over time, the original issue becomes increasingly difficult to recover.

This is why unresolved patterns often continue despite repeated attempts at communication. The structure protects itself—not only through escalation, but through reinterpretation.

And when clarity becomes unstable, interruption becomes difficult, repair becomes limited, and the cycle continues.

Ending Reflections

Patterns that rely on reinterpretation are often difficult to recognize because they do not operate through direct denial alone. Instead, they gradually shift attention away from behavior and toward perception, reaction, emotional framing, or perceived mistreatment. As the focus changes, clarity becomes increasingly difficult to maintain.

In healthy systems, accountability allows conflict to move toward repair. Individuals examine behavior, acknowledge impact, and make adjustments that restore stability. But when accountability threatens the internal structure of a pattern, reinterpretation may begin functioning as psychological protection. The issue is no longer evaluated directly. It is reframed.

Over time, this shift changes the nature of communication itself. Conversations move away from what occurred and toward intention, interpretation, emotional positioning, and narrative defense. The original issue becomes increasingly difficult to recover because the interaction is no longer centered on behavior alone.

This process is often emotionally convincing because it is rarely built entirely from falsehood. Real emotions, past experiences, and genuine pain may all exist within the narrative. The difficulty is not always the presence of emotion, but the displacement of accountability beneath it.

As the pattern repeats, others may begin experiencing confusion, self-doubt, emotional exhaustion, or difficulty maintaining clarity within the interaction. Relationships weaken not only because of conflict itself, but because stable resolution becomes increasingly difficult to sustain.

Real healing requires the ability to tolerate accountability without collapsing into reinterpretation, defensiveness, or role reversal. Stability develops when individuals can remain connected to reality, behavior, and responsibility even when discomfort, shame, or emotional pressure are present.

Ending Quotes

"When interpretation replaces accountability, clarity begins to disappear."
— Levi Sap Nei Thang

"Some patterns survive not through denial, but through reinterpretation."
— Levi Sap Nei Thang

"Role reversal changes the focus of conflict without resolving it."
— Levi Sap Nei Thang

"When reaction becomes the center of conversation, the original issue fades."
— Levi Sap Nei Thang

"Deflection protects patterns by redirecting attention away from behavior."
— Levi Sap Nei Thang

"Emotional intensity can make incomplete narratives feel structurally convincing."
— Levi Sap Nei Thang

Review Questions

1. How does interpretation influence the continuation of recurring behavioral patterns?
2. What is the difference between accountability and deflection?
3. How does role reversal shift the focus of a conflict?

4. Why can emotionally compelling narratives become persuasive even when incomplete?
5. How does emotional amplification affect perception during escalation?
6. In what ways can past experiences reshape interpretation of present situations?
7. Why does clarity become difficult to maintain once the frame of conversation shifts?
8. How can repeated reinterpretation weaken trust and relational stability over time?
9. Why do patterns often protect themselves through narrative rather than direct denial?
10. What role does accountability play in preventing recurring cycles of confusion and escalation?

Chapter 5
The Great Purge
How to Step Away Without Losing Yourself

Opening Quote

"Clarity sometimes requires the courage to stop participating in cycles that never truly resolve."
— Levi Sap Nei Thang

In This Chapter

This chapter focuses on disengagement, boundaries, and the practical process of stepping away from repeated cycles of instability and escalation. It examines how over-engagement unintentionally reinforces destructive patterns and why clarity, consistency, and controlled accountability are essential for long-term emotional protection. Readers will learn how to reduce participation in unresolved cycles without losing compassion, identity, or psychological stability.

Chapter Outline

Chapter Overview

Recognition changes perception.

Once a pattern becomes visible—once it is understood not as a series of isolated events but as a repeating structure—the question is no longer theoretical. It becomes practical.

What do you do with that understanding?

This chapter is not about fixing the pattern or changing the other person. It is about responding with clarity. It is about stepping out of a system that does not resolve, without losing stability, identity, or direction in the process.

The goal is not withdrawal driven by frustration.

It is disengagement guided by understanding.

5.1 Understanding Boundaries

Boundaries are clearly defined emotional, behavioral, or relational limits that protect stability, respect, and personal well-being. Healthy boundaries create structure without hostility and allow relationships to function with clarity and consistency.

5.2 Understanding Disengagement

Disengagement is the intentional reduction of participation in patterns, interactions, or conflicts that repeatedly produce instability or escalation. It is not avoidance based on fear, but a deliberate decision to stop reinforcing unhealthy dynamics.

5.3 Understanding Reinforcement

Reinforcement occurs when responses, attention, or reactions unintentionally strengthen a repeated behavior or pattern. Even negative attention can reinforce conflict if it consistently sustains engagement or emotional intensity.

5.4 Understanding Controlled Accountability

Controlled accountability is the process of addressing behavior directly, clearly, and consistently without emotional escalation. It focuses on defining limits and consequences rather than creating further conflict.

5.5 The Turning Point: From Explanation to Decision

In the earlier stages of interaction, the natural response is explanation.

The individual tries to clarify misunderstandings, improve communication, and resolve conflicts through effort. This approach is effective in environments where both parties are working toward a resolution.

In structural patterns, however, effort does not produce the same outcome.

Explanation is reframed.
Communication is redirected.
The conversation expands without resolving the original issue.

Over time, a realization begins to form.
The issue is not a lack of clarity.
It is a lack of shared structure.

At this point, the question changes.
It is no longer, "How do I explain this better?"
It becomes, "What level of engagement is appropriate?"

This shift marks the beginning of the Great Purge.

5.6 Redefining Responsibility

One of the most difficult aspects of disengagement is redefining responsibility.

For individuals who are empathetic and cooperative, there is often a strong belief that effort can resolve most situations. They take responsibility for maintaining stability, even when the pattern is not within their control.

This belief is not inherently wrong.

It becomes limiting when applied to systems that do not respond to mutual effort.

In such cases, continued engagement may reinforce the pattern rather than resolve it.

Redefining responsibility means recognizing the boundary between what can be influenced and what cannot.

It means understanding that clarity does not require agreement, and stability does not require participation in every interaction.

5.7 The Nature of Boundaries

Boundaries are often misunderstood as barriers.
In reality, they are definitions.

They define where one person's responsibility ends and another's begins.

They establish the conditions under which interaction is appropriate and the limits beyond which it is not.

In stable systems, boundaries are negotiated and respected.
In structural patterns, boundaries may be challenged, reframed, or ignored.

This does not make them ineffective.
It makes them necessary.

A boundary is not an attempt to control another person's behavior.
It is a decision about your own.

It determines how you will respond, what you will participate in, and where you will step back.

5.8 Consistency Over Explanation

In the presence of structural patterns, consistency is more effective than explanation.

Explanation invites interpretation.
It opens the door for the conversation to shift.

Consistency, by contrast, is grounded in action.
It does not argue.
It does not persuade.
It defines.

Over time, consistent behavior establishes clarity in a way that repeated explanation cannot.

It reduces the space in which the pattern can operate.

5.9 Accountability Without Escalation

Disengagement reduces reinforcement.
But in some situations, non-response alone does not interrupt the pattern.

When repeated behavior goes unaddressed, it may be interpreted as acceptance, tolerance, or weakness. In these cases, the pattern can continue—not because it is effective, but because it is not clearly challenged.

This is where accountability becomes necessary.
Accountability is not the same as confrontation.
It does not rely on intensity, volume, or emotional reaction.
It is defined by clarity.

It names the behavior directly, without escalation:

> "This is not acceptable."
> "This pattern is continuing."
> "I will not participate in this."

The goal is not to argue.
The goal is to define.

Clear accountability establishes a boundary that cannot be misinterpreted as silence or agreement.

5.10 When Silence Reinforces the Pattern

Silence can be effective when used deliberately.
But when it replaces clarity, it may unintentionally reinforce the behavior.

If there is no acknowledgment, no boundary, and no consequence, the pattern continues without interruption.

This is not because silence is wrong.
It is because the pattern has not been clearly defined.

In such cases, one direct and controlled response can shift the dynamic more effectively than repeated silence.

5.11 Confrontation vs. Control

Reactive confrontation often escalates the pattern.

It introduces emotion, increases intensity, and creates new material for the cycle to continue.

Controlled confrontation is different.
It is:

- brief
- specific
- non-reactive
- consistent

It does not attempt to win.
It establishes position.

> "This is the boundary."
> "This will not continue."

After that, consistency—not repetition—is what maintains it.

5.12 The Balance

Effective response requires balance.
Too much engagement reinforces the pattern.
Too little clarity allows it to continue.
The goal is not a constant response.
It is a precise response.
Define once.
Maintain consistently.

Disengage when necessary.
Over time, this balance reduces both escalation and ambiguity.

5.13 Where the Pattern Appears

The pattern described in this book is not limited to a single environment.

It can appear across many contexts.

In public-facing roles, it may be expressed through repeated criticism, ongoing opposition, or a focus on conflict-driven narratives.

In online spaces, it may appear as constant verbal confrontation, recurring disputes, or a pattern of engaging through argument rather than dialogue.

In workplaces, it may take the form of repeated interpersonal conflict, resistance to boundaries, or ongoing tension within teams.

In educational settings, similar dynamics may emerge through peer conflict, division, or recurring escalation in interaction.

The setting may change.
But the underlying structure remains consistent.

5.14 Recognizing the Pattern Across Contexts

It is important to understand that these behaviors are not defined by profession, role, or status.

They are defined by repetition.

The same patterns can appear in different environments, with different individuals, and at different levels of visibility.

What matters is not where the behavior occurs, but how consistently it follows the same structure.

5.15 Choosing Distance

Not all patterns need to be engaged.
In some cases, the most appropriate response is distance.
This is not avoidance out of fear.
It is a selection based on awareness.

It is possible to recognize a pattern, understand its direction, and choose not to participate in it.

Different people are shaped by different environments.

Differences in upbringing, experience, and exposure are part of human variation.

Understanding this does not require acceptance of harmful patterns.
It allows for clarity.
And clarity allows for choice.

5.16 Disengagement as Clarity

Disengagement is often misunderstood as avoidance.

In this context, it is clarity.

When engagement consistently leads to escalation, confusion, or instability, reducing participation becomes a way of limiting reinforcement.

This does not require complete separation in every case.

It may involve adjusting how you interact, how often you engage, and what you choose to respond to.

The goal is not to remove yourself from all interaction.
It is to remove yourself from patterns that do not resolve.

5.17 The Internal Challenge of Letting Go

Even when the pattern is clear, disengagement is not immediate.

There is investment—time, energy, emotional alignment. There is also the memory of how the interaction began, particularly during earlier phases of care, attention, and connection.

This creates hesitation.

The individual may feel that stepping away means abandoning something that once felt meaningful. They may question whether they have done enough to resolve the situation.

This is where clarity is essential.
The decision to disengage is not based on a single moment.
It is based on repeated patterns.

5.18 Managing the Pull to Re-Engage

Once disengagement begins, there is often a pull to re-engage.

This pull may come from habit, from a desire to restore clarity, or from the belief that one more conversation might change the outcome.

This is a natural response.

But it must be evaluated against the pattern.

If repeated engagement has not produced a resolution, additional engagement is unlikely to do so.

Recognizing this allows the individual to maintain consistency.

5.19 The Role of Silence

Silence, in this context, is not passive.
It is selective.

It is the decision not to respond to every statement, not to engage with every escalation, and not to correct every interpretation.

This does not mean ignoring important issues.
It means choosing when engagement is productive.
Silence reduces reinforcement.
Without consistent response, the pattern has less material to operate on.

5.20 Perception and Misinterpretation

Disengagement may change how others perceive the situation.

In environments where narratives have shifted, stepping back may be interpreted in different ways. It may be seen as agreement, avoidance, or confirmation of an existing narrative.

These interpretations are not always controllable.
Attempting to correct every perception can reintroduce the pattern.
Clarity, in this stage, is internal.
It is maintained through consistency rather than constant explanation.
Over time, stable behavior becomes more visible than reactive engagement.

5.21 Escalation Through Accusation

As disengagement becomes consistent, the pattern does not always fade quietly. In some cases, it escalates.

When direct engagement no longer produces the same response, the individual may shift strategies. Instead of continuing the original interaction, they may introduce more serious or emotionally charged accusations in an attempt to regain attention, control the narrative, or force re-engagement.

These accusations may take different forms depending on the context.

They may involve claims of unfair treatment, exclusion, bias, or intentional harm. The specific language may vary, but the underlying function remains the same: to reframe disengagement as wrongdoing.

This creates pressure.

The individual who has stepped back may feel compelled to respond—not because the original pattern has changed, but because the new accusation carries greater weight. Silence may now feel risky. Engagement may feel unavoidable.

This is where clarity becomes essential.

Not every accusation requires an immediate response. Not every escalation reflects the original issue. In many cases, the accusation is not an isolated concern—it is a continuation of the pattern in a different form.

Understanding this distinction allows the individual to respond deliberately rather than reactively.

The goal is not to ignore legitimate concerns.

It is to recognize when escalation is being used to pull you back into a cycle that does not resolve.

5.22 Protection Without Reaction

As patterns intensify, disengagement may not always be accepted quietly.

In some situations, stepping back is reframed as wrongdoing. The individual may face accusations of bias, exclusion, or unfair treatment. These accusations can carry emotional weight and may create pressure to re-engage, defend, or justify the decision to step away.

This is where clarity must remain steady.
Disengagement is not the same as discrimination.
Boundaries are not the same as rejection.

Choosing distance from a repeated pattern is not a statement about identity—it is a decision about behavior and stability.

When the pattern is clearly recognized, the focus must not shift.
The issue is not who the person is.
The issue is what the pattern produces.

If engagement consistently leads to escalation, confusion, or instability, then reducing that engagement is a rational and necessary response.

This does not require hostility.
It does not require public defense.
It does not require ongoing justification.
It requires consistency.

Maintaining distance from patterns that do not resolve is not avoidance—it is protection.

Over time, this consistency becomes more powerful than any explanation.

5.23 Protecting What Remains Stable

As disengagement progresses, attention shifts to what remains stable.
Relationships that are not part of the pattern.
Work that is constructive.
Environments that support consistency.
Protecting these areas becomes a priority.
This does not require isolation.
It requires alignment.
The individual invests energy in what builds rather than what repeats.

5.24 Reclaiming Direction

One of the most significant outcomes of disengagement is the recovery of direction.

When attention is no longer consumed by unresolved patterns, it becomes available for other areas of life.

Focus returns to personal goals, stable relationships, and constructive work.

This shift is gradual.
It develops as the pattern loses its central position.
Over time, the individual is no longer organized around the conflict.
They are organized around their own direction.

5.25 Emotional Recalibration

As engagement decreases, emotional responses begin to change.
Situations that once triggered strong reactions may feel less urgent.
The need to respond immediately diminishes.
The emotional intensity of the pattern reduces.
This is not suppression.
It is recalibration.
The individual is no longer reacting automatically.
They are choosing when and how to respond.

5.26 The Core Principle

The Great Purge is not about eliminating the pattern.
It is about removing yourself from its reinforcement.
You are not responsible for stopping the pattern.
You are responsible for how you engage with it.

Ending Reflections

Recognition alone does not interrupt a pattern.

Understanding how a cycle operates is important, but awareness without behavioral change often leads to continued participation in the same instability. Lasting change begins when clarity becomes action.

One of the most difficult realizations is understanding that not every pattern responds to explanation, emotional investment, patience, or repeated attempts at repair. In stable systems, communication strengthens understanding. In unresolved structural patterns, communication may instead become absorbed into escalation, reinterpretation, or continued conflict.

This is why boundaries become essential.

Boundaries are not acts of punishment, hostility, or emotional withdrawal. They are structures that protect clarity, stability, emotional health, and personal direction. They define what an individual will participate in, what they will reinforce, and where engagement must end in order for stability to remain possible.

Disengagement is therefore not always avoidance. In many situations, it is the deliberate refusal to continue reinforcing cycles that repeatedly produce confusion, escalation, emotional exhaustion, or instability. The goal is not to control another person's behavior. The goal is to regain responsibility for one's own participation.

Over time, consistent boundaries reduce emotional reactivity. The pressure to respond immediately weakens. Attention gradually shifts away from unresolved conflict and toward what remains constructive, stable, and meaningful.

Healing often begins not when the pattern changes, but when the individual stops organizing life around it.

Real clarity develops when individuals learn that protecting peace, direction, emotional regulation, and long-term stability is not abandonment. It is discernment.

Ending Quotes

"Not every conflict deserves continued participation."
— Levi Sap Nei Thang

"Boundaries protect stability when explanation no longer produces clarity."
— Levi Sap Nei Thang

"Disengagement is not surrender. It is selective participation."
— Levi Sap Nei Thang

"Repeated engagement can unintentionally strengthen unresolved patterns."
— Levi Sap Nei Thang

"Consistency establishes clarity more effectively than repeated argument."
— Levi Sap Nei Thang

"Stepping away from instability is sometimes the beginning of emotional recovery."
— Levi Sap Nei Thang

"Clarity is maintained through consistency, not constant defense."
— Levi Sap Nei Thang

"You are not required to remain inside cycles that repeatedly refuse repair."
— Levi Sap Nei Thang

Key Insight

Not every pattern can be resolved through continued engagement. In some situations, clarity, boundaries, and intentional disengagement become necessary forms of emotional protection and long-term stability.

Summary

This chapter examined the practical process of stepping away from repeated cycles of instability, escalation, and unresolved conflict without losing emotional stability, compassion, or personal direction. It explored how continued over-engagement can unintentionally reinforce destructive patterns and why boundaries, consistency, controlled accountability, and selective disengagement are essential for long-term clarity and protection.

The chapter explained how individuals often begin by attempting to resolve instability through repeated explanation, emotional investment, or increased effort. However, in structural patterns where communication is repeatedly redirected or escalated, the issue eventually shifts from improving understanding to determining appropriate levels of engagement.

The chapter also examined the role of boundaries as structures that define participation rather than punish others. It explored the difference between reactive confrontation and controlled accountability, showing how calm, direct, and consistent responses are often more effective than repeated emotional engagement or argument.

In addition, the chapter addressed the emotional difficulty of disengagement itself, including the pull to re-engage, the fear of misunderstanding, and the pressure created by escalating accusations or narrative shifts. It emphasized that disengagement is not avoidance based on fear, but a deliberate refusal to continue reinforcing cycles that repeatedly produce confusion, instability, or emotional exhaustion.

Ultimately, the chapter demonstrated that healing and recovery begin when individuals stop organizing life around unresolved conflict and begin reorganizing attention toward stability, emotional regulation, constructive relationships, and personal direction. Real clarity develops not through controlling others, but through consistent participation in what builds rather than what repeatedly destabilizes.

Conclusion

You cannot always change what you encounter.
But you can change how you engage with it.
Recognition alone does not interrupt a pattern.

What changes the outcome is consistency—clear boundaries, controlled accountability, selective engagement, and the willingness to stop reinforcing cycles that repeatedly produce instability.

Disengagement is not weakness.

It is the decision to protect clarity, stability, emotional health, and direction when repeated interaction no longer produces repair.

Over time, distance creates perspective. Perspective restores balance. And balance allows the individual to reorganize life around what builds rather than what continuously destabilizes.

Clarity is not control.
It is direction.

Review Questions

1. Why does recognition of a pattern not automatically interrupt it?
2. How can repeated explanation unintentionally reinforce unresolved conflict structures?
3. What is the difference between reactive confrontation and controlled accountability?

4. Why are boundaries necessary in environments shaped by repeated escalation or instability?
5. How can silence both reduce and unintentionally reinforce a pattern depending on context?
6. Why is consistency often more effective than repeated argument or emotional persuasion?
7. What role does disengagement play in protecting emotional stability and clarity?
8. How can individuals maintain compassion while still choosing distance from harmful patterns?
9. Why may escalation intensify when disengagement becomes consistent?
10. What does it mean to reclaim direction after stepping away from repeated cycles of instability?

PART II

The Damage of Unhealed Survival

Chapter 6
The Poverty of the Soul
When Survival Never Heals

Opening Quote

"Poverty can wound the body, but bitterness wounds the heart."
— Levi Sap Nei Thang

In This Chapter

This chapter explores how prolonged emotional survival can create an internal poverty that continues long after external hardship ends. It examines survival mentality, emotional scarcity, chronic insecurity, fear of loss, hypervigilance, emotional numbness, transactional relationships, and the inability to feel safe, restful, or emotionally fulfilled even after material conditions improve. The chapter also discusses how healing requires more than escaping hardship physically; it requires restoring the emotional life that survival slowly damaged.

Chapter Outline

Opening Reflection
Chapter Overview
6.1 When Survival Becomes Identity
6.2 The Scarcity Mentality
6.3 Hypervigilance — Living as Though Danger Never Left
6.4 Emotional Numbness and the Loss of Joy
6.5 Transactional Relationships and Emotional Insecurity
6.6 The Fear of Rest
6.7 When External Success Cannot Heal Internal Poverty
6.8 Healing the Poverty of the Soul
6.9 Learning How to Live Instead of Merely Survive
Key Insight
Summary
Conclusion
Ending Reflection
Ending Quotes
Review Questions

Opening Reflection

Some people escape poverty physically but never escape it emotionally.

Their circumstances may improve.

They may become successful, stable, educated, respected, or financially secure. Yet internally, they continue living as though danger is always near.

Rest feels unsafe.
Trust feels risky.
Generosity feels threatening.
Peace feels temporary.
The body survived.
But the soul never stopped surviving.

Long periods of hardship often train the nervous system to focus entirely on protection, scarcity, endurance, and survival. These adaptations may help a person endure difficult environments, but when survival mode never turns off, emotional life slowly becomes restricted.

Joy becomes difficult.
Trust weakens.
Relationships become transactional.
Rest produces guilt.
Fear quietly controls decision-making.

Even abundance feels emotionally fragile because the mind remains psychologically attached to loss.

This chapter explores the hidden poverty that exists beyond money — the poverty of emotional safety, inner peace, trust, emotional fullness, and spiritual rest.

Some people survive life without ever truly learning how to live it.

Chapter Overview

Human beings are designed not only to survive physically but also to experience emotional security, connection, peace, meaning, and psychological stability. However, prolonged exposure to hardship, deprivation, instability, neglect, fear, or emotional insecurity often forces individuals into chronic survival mode.

Survival mode changes behavior.

The nervous system becomes highly focused on protection, scarcity management, emotional vigilance, and threat anticipation. While these adaptations may initially preserve survival, they can later become emotionally destructive if they remain active long after danger has passed.

This chapter examines how unresolved survival conditioning produces emotional poverty even in people whose external circumstances improved significantly. It explores fear-based living, emotional emptiness, distrust, exhaustion, scarcity mentality, and the inability to emotionally experience safety or fulfillment.

Most importantly, this chapter explains that healing requires more than escaping external poverty. True healing involves restoring the emotional and spiritual parts of the self that survival quietly suppressed for years.

6.1 When Survival Becomes Identity

Survival is meant to be temporary.
But for some individuals, survival eventually becomes identity.

People raised in environments of chronic instability, deprivation, emotional neglect, violence, fear, or insecurity often develop psychological systems organized entirely around endurance. The mind becomes trained to expect hardship constantly.

As a result, the individual may unconsciously define themselves through struggle:

- surviving,
- enduring,
- protecting,
- sacrificing,
- or preparing for disaster.

Even after life improves externally, the nervous system may continue functioning as though danger is still present.

The person may feel unable to relax fully because emotional safety never become psychologically familiar.

Rest feels irresponsible.
Vulnerability feels dangerous.

Receiving help feels uncomfortable because survival taught them that dependence creates risk.

Over time, survival stops being a temporary state and becomes a permanent emotional posture toward life.

The person no longer knows how to exist without preparing for emotional collapse.

6.2 The Scarcity Mentality

One of the strongest effects of prolonged hardship is scarcity mentality.
Scarcity mentality occurs when the mind becomes psychologically organized around fear of not having enough:

- enough money,
- enough safety,
- enough stability,
- enough love,
- enough opportunity,
- or enough emotional security.

Even when circumstances improve, the fear often remains.

A person may become chronically anxious about losing what they have. They may hoard emotionally, financially, or relationally because loss feels psychologically catastrophic. Generosity becomes difficult because giving feels unsafe. Trusting abundance feels dangerous because survival conditioned the mind to expect deprivation.

Scarcity mentality also affects emotional relationships.

Some individuals cling to relationships out of fear of abandonment rather than genuine emotional health. Others become excessively controlling because uncertainty feels intolerable. Some remain emotionally defensive because they subconsciously believe emotional safety can disappear at any moment.

The external hardship may have ended years ago.

But internally, the nervous system still behaves as though survival resources are dangerously limited.

6.3 Hypervigilance — Living as Though Danger Never Left

Many individuals who endured prolonged hardship develop chronic hypervigilance.

Hypervigilance is a persistent state of psychological alertness in which the nervous system continuously scans for danger, rejection, humiliation, instability, or loss.

The person may struggle to feel calm even during peaceful situations.

They may overanalyze conversations, anticipate betrayal, prepare constantly for worst-case scenarios, or remain emotionally tense even when no immediate threat exists. Small uncertainties trigger disproportionate anxiety because the nervous system learned that unpredictability often preceded pain.

For some individuals, peace itself begins feeling unfamiliar.

When the body remains trapped in long-term survival conditioning, emotional stillness can actually feel uncomfortable.

Chaos becomes familiar.
Calmness feels suspicious.

This is one reason some emotionally wounded individuals unconsciously recreate instability in relationships, work environments, or emotional situations. Their nervous system has adapted so strongly to survival mode that emotional peace feels psychologically unnatural.

6.4 Emotional Numbness and the Loss of Joy

Survival often requires emotional suppression.

In difficult environments, people sometimes learn to disconnect from emotional pain simply to continue functioning. Over time, however, this emotional shutdown may extend beyond pain alone.

The person stops feeling fully alive emotionally.

Joy becomes muted. Excitement weakens. Emotional warmth decreases. Life becomes centered primarily around responsibility, endurance, and emotional survival rather than meaning, creativity, connection, or peace.

Some individuals become so focused on surviving that they forget how to experience simple emotional presence.

They may constantly think:

- about the next problem,
- the next bill,
- the next danger,
- the next conflict,
- or the next crisis.

The nervous system remains future-focused and threat-focused.

As a result, even beautiful moments become emotionally inaccessible because the mind never fully leaves survival mode long enough to experience them.

This creates a quiet internal emptiness that many people struggle to explain.

Externally, life may appear stable.
Internally, emotional life feels absent.

6.5 Transactional Relationships and Emotional Insecurity

People shaped by prolonged survival sometimes begin viewing relationships transactionally.

This does not necessarily happen out of selfishness. Often it develops because survival taught them that safety depends upon usefulness, performance, sacrifice, or emotional bargaining.

The individual may unconsciously believe:

- love must be earned,
- kindness always carries hidden conditions,
- vulnerability creates danger,
- or relationships exist primarily for survival support rather than emotional connection.

As a result, trust becomes difficult.

The person may constantly question:

> "What does this person really want from me?"
> "Will they leave if I fail?"
> "Am I only valuable when I provide something?"

This survival-based relational thinking weakens emotional intimacy because the relationship becomes organized around fear instead of emotional safety.

The person may deeply desire love while simultaneously struggling to believe genuine love exists without conditions.

6.6 The Fear of Rest

Many survival-conditioned individuals struggle profoundly with rest.

When a person spends years fighting instability, emotional stillness may feel psychologically dangerous. Rest creates vulnerability because survival required constant alertness and productivity.

As a result, some individuals feel guilty when resting.

They may become uncomfortable during peace, free time, silence, or emotional stillness. Productivity becomes emotionally fused with worth and safety. Slowing down triggers anxiety because the nervous system fears losing control.

Some individuals unconsciously believe:

> "If I stop struggling, something bad will happen."

This mindset creates chronic exhaustion.

Even success does not bring emotional relief because the nervous system never learned how to feel secure without constant striving.

The body survives.
But the soul remains exhausted.

6.7 When External Success Cannot Heal Internal Poverty

Some individuals eventually achieve financial success, education, recognition, or external stability but still feel emotionally empty internally.

This creates confusion because they expected success to remove the emotional suffering created during hardship.

However, external improvement alone cannot heal internal survival conditioning.

A person may:

- earn more money,
- buy a home,
- gain status,
- build a career,
- or escape physical poverty,

while still carrying:

- fear,
- insecurity,

- emotional emptiness,
- distrust,
- bitterness,
- or chronic emotional tension internally.

The wound was never only financial.
It was emotional, psychological, relational, and spiritual.

This explains why some externally successful individuals continue feeling internally restless or emotionally deprived despite material achievement.

Survival preserved their external life.
But survival never healed the internal life.

6.8 Healing the Poverty of the Soul

Healing begins when survival is no longer treated as the final goal of life.

A person must eventually move beyond merely avoiding destruction and begin rebuilding emotional life itself.

This process often requires:

- emotional safety,
- self-reflection,
- counseling,
- spiritual restoration,
- emotionally healthy relationships,
- gratitude,
- learning to trust,
- and relearning rest.

The nervous system must gradually experience stability repeatedly before emotional safety begins feeling believable again.

Healing also involves grieving what survival stole:

- lost peace,
- lost childhood,
- lost trust,
- lost emotional innocence,
- or years spent living in fear.

Many survival-conditioned individuals never allowed themselves to grieve because survival demanded constant endurance.

But healing requires acknowledging the emotional cost honestly.

"Come to me, all who are weary and burdened, and I will give you rest."
— Matthew 11:28

Rest is not laziness.
For the survival-conditioned soul, rest is healing.

6.9 Learning How to Live Instead of Merely Survive

One of the final stages of healing is learning that life is meant to contain more than endurance.

Many survival-conditioned individuals know how to struggle but do not know how to live peacefully. They know how to survive hardship but not how to experience emotional fullness safely.

Healing teaches the nervous system that:

- peace is not weakness,
- rest is not danger,
- vulnerability is not always destruction,
- and emotional safety can exist.

Over time, the person slowly stops organizing life entirely around fear, scarcity, and protection.

The soul begins opening again.
Joy returns gradually.
Trust becomes possible.
Relationships feel less transactional.
Emotional breathing becomes easier.
The individual finally realizes:

> "I survived.
> But now I must learn how to live."

Key Insight

Some people escape external poverty while remaining emotionally imprisoned by survival mode internally.

The deepest poverty is not always material deprivation.

Sometimes it is the inability to feel safe, peaceful, emotionally alive, or spiritually rested even after survival is no longer necessary.

Summary

This chapter explored how prolonged hardship and chronic survival mode can create a lasting internal poverty that continues long after external circumstances improve. It examined survival identity, scarcity mentality, hypervigilance, emotional numbness, transactional relationships, fear of rest, and the inability of external success alone to heal emotional deprivation.

The chapter also discussed emotional restoration, grieving survival-related losses, and the gradual process of learning how to live peacefully instead of merely surviving constantly.

Conclusion

Survival can preserve life while quietly starving the soul.

Many people spend years escaping hardship physically while never realizing that emotionally, psychologically, and spiritually, they are still living inside the same fear-based survival system.

The body may have escaped poverty.
But the nervous system never stopped preparing for disaster.

Healing begins when a person realizes they deserve more than mere survival. Human beings were not created only to endure fear endlessly. They were also created for peace, connection, rest, meaning, and emotional fullness.

The deepest healing occurs when survival finally loosens its grip on the soul.

Ending Reflection

Some wounds are invisible because they do not appear in financial records, physical scars, or public achievements. They appear quietly in the inability to rest, trust, feel safe, or experience joy fully.

Many survival-conditioned individuals become highly functional externally while remaining emotionally exhausted internally. They continue carrying fear long after danger has passed because survival became emotionally permanent.

But the human soul was not designed to live forever in emergency mode.

Healing begins when a person stops measuring life only by survival and starts asking whether the heart itself has ever truly felt peace.

Surviving life is not the same as living it.

Ending Quotes

"Come to me, all who are weary and burdened, and I will give you rest."
— Matthew 11:28

"Some people survive poverty financially while remaining emotionally poor in safety, trust, and peace."
— Levi Sap Nei Thang

"Survival protected the body, but healing must restore the soul."
— Levi Sap Nei Thang

"The deepest exhaustion is not physical fatigue. It is a soul that never learned it was finally safe."
— Levi Sap Nei Thang

Review Questions

1. How can survival become an emotional identity?
2. What is scarcity mentality, and how does it continue after hardship ends?
3. Why do some individuals remain hypervigilant even during peaceful situations?
4. How does prolonged survival affect emotional joy and connection?
5. Why do some survival-conditioned individuals struggle with trust and intimacy?
6. What role does fear play in transactional relationships?
7. Why can external success fail to heal internal emotional poverty?
8. Why do many survival-conditioned individuals struggle with rest?
9. What does it mean to move from survival into emotional living?

Chapter 6: The Poverty of the Soul

Chapter 7
The Bitter Heart

Opening Quote

"See to it that no bitter root grows up to cause trouble and defile many."
— Hebrews 12:15

In This Chapter

This chapter explores the emotional and psychological development of bitterness, how unresolved pain slowly reshapes personality and perception, and why bitterness often spreads into relationships, communication, and behavior. It also examines resentment, emotional fixation, chronic anger, envy, and emotional exhaustion, while discussing the possibility of emotional restoration before bitterness fully consumes the heart.

Chapter Outline

Opening Reflection

Bitterness rarely begins as bitterness.

It usually begins as disappointment, humiliation, betrayal, neglect, rejection, unfairness, or unresolved emotional pain. At first, the wound may appear temporary. The person tells themselves they will eventually move on. But when pain remains unresolved for long periods of time, it slowly changes emotional perception.

The mind begins replaying injuries repeatedly.
Trust weakens.
Irritation increases.
Compassion slowly decreases.

Eventually, the person no longer responds only to the original wound. The wound begins responding through them.

A bitter heart is not simply an angry heart. It is often a wounded heart that remained emotionally trapped in unresolved pain for too long.

This chapter explores how bitterness develops, how it reshapes emotional behavior, and why healing must occur before resentment becomes a permanent emotional identity.

Chapter Overview

Bitterness is one of the most psychologically destructive emotional conditions because it quietly transforms perception, relationships, communication, and emotional stability over time. Unlike temporary anger, bitterness often becomes chronic. It attaches itself to memory, identity, and worldview.

A bitter person may begin interpreting life primarily through disappointment and resentment. Emotional pain gradually becomes emotionally organizing. Small frustrations trigger large reactions because the nervous system remains internally burdened by unresolved emotional injuries.

This chapter examines the emotional roots of bitterness, the behavioral patterns associated with it, and the internal exhaustion it creates. It also explores how bitterness spreads into families, friendships, workplaces, and communities when left unresolved.

Most importantly, this chapter explains that bitterness is not irreversible. Emotional restoration remains possible when individuals become willing to confront pain honestly instead of feeding resentment continuously.

7.1 The Root of Bitterness

Bitterness usually develops when emotional pain remains unresolved for long periods of time.

The original injury may involve betrayal, rejection, humiliation, abandonment, injustice, emotional neglect, manipulation, chronic criticism, or repeated disappointment. In many cases, the person initially suppresses the emotional pain rather than processing it directly.

Externally, they may appear functional.
Internally, however, unresolved resentment continues growing quietly.

Over time, the mind repeatedly returns to the injury.
Conversations are mentally replayed.
Past humiliations remain emotionally active.
Old betrayals continue triggering emotional reactions years later.
Instead of fading naturally, the pain becomes psychologically embedded.

Eventually, bitterness stops attaching only to the original event.
It begins influencing the person's entire emotional outlook.
Eventually, the person no longer responds only to the original wound.
The wound begins responding through them.

The individual may become increasingly cynical, suspicious, emotionally reactive, or emotionally exhausted. They begin expecting disappointment before it occurs because disappointment has become emotionally familiar.

"See to it that no bitter root grows up to cause trouble and defile many."
— Hebrews 12:15

The phrase "bitter root" is psychologically powerful because bitterness behaves very much like a root system. It spreads beneath the surface long before its full effects become visible externally.

7.2 How Bitterness Changes Perception

One of the most dangerous aspects of bitterness is that it gradually alters perception itself.

A bitter person often begins interpreting neutral situations negatively. Small misunderstandings feel like personal attacks. Other people's success may trigger irritation instead of celebration. Trust becomes increasingly difficult because the mind constantly anticipates harm, disrespect, or disappointment.

Over time, bitterness creates emotional filtering. The individual unconsciously notices negative experiences more intensely than positive ones. Emotional injuries receive constant mental attention while moments of peace, kindness, or stability become psychologically minimized.

This distorted perception can eventually affect every relationship.

Friends may feel emotionally exhausted around the bitter person.

Conversations become dominated by resentment, criticism, negativity, or unresolved grievances. Even ordinary interactions begin carrying emotional tension because bitterness continuously searches for confirmation of its own worldview.

The painful irony is that bitterness often creates the very isolation the person fears most.

As emotional negativity increases, healthy relationships may weaken, creating even greater loneliness and resentment.

7.3 The Emotional Addiction to Resentment

Some individuals become emotionally attached to resentment without realizing it.

This does not mean they enjoy suffering consciously.
Rather, resentment gradually becomes emotionally familiar.

The mind repeatedly returns to anger because anger temporarily creates a feeling of emotional control or justification.

The person may mentally rehearse past injuries constantly:

- what was said,
- what was unfair,
- what should have happened,
- or how they were wronged.

Over time, resentment becomes psychologically consuming.

Instead of processing pain and moving forward, the individual remains emotionally anchored to the injury. Their emotional energy becomes organized around unresolved conflict.

This often produces chronic emotional exhaustion. The nervous system remains activated for extended periods, leaving the person mentally tired, emotionally reactive, and internally restless.

Bitterness eventually steals emotional peace even when external conflict is absent.

7.4 When Bitterness Spreads to Others

Bitterness rarely remains isolated inside one individual.

Unhealed resentment often spreads outward into communication, parenting, friendships, workplaces, marriages, and social environments. A bitter person may unintentionally create emotional instability around others through constant criticism, hostility, emotional harshness, or negativity.

Children raised around chronic bitterness may develop emotional anxiety or defensive communication patterns. Relationships gradually weaken under repeated emotional tension. Even supportive people may eventually distance themselves because constant resentment becomes emotionally draining.

In many situations, bitterness reproduces itself across generations. Individuals who grew up surrounded by emotional hostility sometimes unconsciously repeat similar patterns later in life because bitterness became normalized emotionally.

This is why emotional healing is not merely personal. It also affects families, communities, and future relationships.

Unresolved bitterness often becomes contagious emotionally.

7.5 Envy, Comparison, and the Bitter Heart

Bitterness often grows stronger through comparison.

A person who feels emotionally wounded or disappointed may begin constantly comparing their life to others. Other people's happiness, success, relationships, opportunities, or recognition may trigger hidden resentment.

Instead of feeling inspired, the bitter heart feels aggravated.

The individual may begin asking internally:

"Why them and not me?"
"Why was my life harder?"
"Why do others seem happy while I continue suffering?"

Comparison deepens emotional dissatisfaction because the person becomes increasingly focused on perceived unfairness.

Social comparison is especially dangerous because it convinces the individual that peace is impossible unless life becomes equal to someone else's circumstances. Instead of developing gratitude or emotional acceptance, the person remains psychologically trapped in resentment.

Envy and bitterness often strengthen one another.

The more a person compares, the more bitterness grows. The more bitterness grows, the more comparison intensifies.

7.6 Bitterness and Jealousy

Bitterness rarely remains limited to past pain alone.

Over time, unresolved resentment may begin shaping how individuals perceive the success, happiness, stability, or opportunities of others.

Instead of feeling inspired, the bitter heart may feel threatened, irritated, resentful, or emotionally disturbed by the progress of other people.

Jealousy often develops when unresolved pain combines with comparison.

- The person may silently think:
- "Why do they have what I never had?"
- "Why are they loved while I suffered?"
- "Why do good things happen to them instead of me?"
- "Life was never fair to me."

Over time, jealousy can distort perception.

The bitter individual may begin minimizing others' achievements, criticizing people unfairly, attacking reputations, sabotaging relationships, or secretly resenting those who display happiness, peace, confidence, stability, or success.

In severe cases, the individual may experience emotional satisfaction when others fail because another person's success unconsciously intensifies their own unresolved emotional pain.

Bitterness and jealousy often reinforce one another.

The more comparison increases, the deeper resentment grows.

The deeper resentment grows, the more difficult gratitude, peace, emotional healing, and genuine happiness become.

This does not mean every jealous thought makes a person deeply bitter. Human beings naturally experience moments of comparison and insecurity.

The danger develops when jealousy becomes chronic, emotionally justified, and repeatedly nurtured instead of confronted honestly.

Healing requires learning to celebrate the well-being of others without interpreting another person's success as personal rejection, humiliation, or proof of personal failure.

Gratitude, emotional accountability, forgiveness, and internal healing help weaken the cycle of resentment and comparison that bitterness often creates.

7.7 The Physical and Emotional Cost of Bitterness

Bitterness affects more than emotions alone.

Chronic resentment often produces physical and psychological consequences over time. The body is not designed to remain in prolonged emotional hostility continuously. Extended emotional stress can contribute to fatigue, sleep disturbance, irritability, anxiety, emotional exhaustion, and difficulty experiencing calmness.

Mentally, bitterness narrows emotional flexibility. Joy becomes harder to experience. Peace feels unfamiliar. Relaxation may even feel uncomfortable because the nervous system has adapted to emotional tension.

Many bitter individuals become trapped in constant internal vigilance. Even during peaceful moments, the mind remains emotionally prepared for disappointment or conflict.

This state becomes exhausting.

The person may eventually feel emotionally empty, disconnected, or chronically dissatisfied without fully understanding why.

Bitterness consumes emotional energy while offering no true emotional restoration in return.

7.8 The Difference Between Grief and Bitterness

Not all emotional pain is bitterness.

Healthy grief acknowledges loss honestly while still allowing emotional movement and healing over time. Bitterness, however, keeps emotional pain psychologically frozen.

Grief says:

> "This hurt me deeply."

Bitterness says:

> "I will carry this injury forever."

Grief allows sadness to move gradually toward acceptance. Bitterness continually reactivates emotional injury through resentment and fixation.

This distinction is important because emotionally wounded people sometimes fear healing itself. They worry that releasing bitterness somehow minimizes the seriousness of what happened.

But healing does not erase injustice.
Healing simply prevents injustice from permanently controlling emotional life.

7.9 Healing the Bitter Heart

Healing bitterness requires emotional honesty.

A person must first recognize the resentment they are carrying instead of continuously justifying it internally. Many bitter individuals focus entirely on what others did wrong while ignoring how resentment itself is now damaging their own emotional well-being.

Healing often begins with acknowledging:

- the pain,
- the anger,
- the disappointment,

and the emotional exhaustion honestly.

From there, emotional restoration gradually becomes possible through forgiveness, gratitude, emotional boundaries, counseling, prayer, self-reflection, and healthier emotional environments.

"Create in me a clean heart, O God, and renew a right spirit within me."
— Psalm 51:10

Healing does not happen instantly. Deep resentment formed over many years often requires time, repetition, and emotional restructuring.

But the bitter heart is not beyond restoration.

People can heal. Emotional patterns can change. The heart can soften again without becoming naïve.

7.10 Peace Feels Strange to the Bitter Heart

One difficult reality of healing is that peace initially feels unfamiliar to deeply bitter individuals.

After living in emotional tension for long periods, calmness may feel emotionally uncomfortable at first. Some individuals unconsciously recreate conflict because emotional chaos feels more familiar than stability.

This is why healing often requires learning how to tolerate peace.

The nervous system must gradually relearn emotional safety, emotional stillness, and emotional regulation. This process may feel unnatural initially because bitterness trained the mind to remain emotionally alert constantly.

Over time, however, peace becomes less threatening and more emotionally sustainable.

The healed person eventually realizes that emotional stability is not weakness.

It is freedom.

7.11 Survival-Based Narcissistic Traits

In some individuals, prolonged survival conditioning, unresolved bitterness, humiliation, emotional deprivation, or chronic insecurity may gradually contribute to the development of narcissistic behavioral patterns.

Because survival becomes psychologically centered around self-protection, control, validation, status, or emotional defense, empathy for others may slowly weaken over time.

The individual may become increasingly self-focused, emotionally defensive, entitled, manipulative, attention-seeking, or dismissive of the emotional needs of others.

In some cases, other people begin existing primarily as tools for validation, financial advancement, emotional control, admiration, or personal benefit rather than as individuals deserving mutual care and respect.

This does not mean every wounded or financially struggling person develops narcissistic traits. Many people remain compassionate despite severe hardship.

However, when bitterness, shame, resentment, insecurity, humiliation, and survival thinking remain unresolved for long periods, narcissistic tendencies may emerge as psychological defense mechanisms designed to protect a fragile sense of worth, control, or identity.

Underneath the external confidence, dominance, or emotional hardness, there often remains unresolved fear, insecurity, shame, emotional deprivation, or fear of powerlessness.

Key Insight

Bitterness does not only remember pain.

It allows pain to continue controlling emotional perception, behavior, relationships, and identity long after the original injury occurred.

Healing begins when a person stops feeding resentment and starts pursuing emotional restoration instead.

Summary

This chapter explored how bitterness develops through unresolved emotional pain and gradually reshapes emotional perception, relationships, communication, and psychological stability. It examined resentment, emotional fixation, comparison, envy, chronic negativity, and the emotional exhaustion associated with prolonged bitterness.

The chapter also distinguished grief from bitterness and explained how healing becomes possible through emotional honesty, forgiveness, gratitude, self-reflection, and emotional restoration. Ultimately, bitterness is not simply anger maintained over time; it is unresolved pain that has begun controlling the heart.

Conclusion

A bitter heart is often a wounded heart that remained trapped in pain for too long.

Without healing, resentment slowly spreads into perception, relationships, personality, and emotional behavior. What began as injury gradually becomes identity.

But bitterness is not irreversible.

The human heart is capable of restoration when pain is confronted honestly instead of continuously feeding resentment. A person can suffer deeply without remaining emotionally imprisoned by suffering forever.

Healing begins when the heart finally becomes more committed to peace than to resentment.

Ending Reflection

Bitterness promises protection, but eventually produces isolation, exhaustion, and emotional heaviness. It convinces the wounded person that resentment will somehow heal the injury, yet resentment often deepens the wound instead.

Many bitter individuals are not evil people. They are hurting people who remained emotionally trapped in unresolved pain for too long. The danger arises when pain becomes emotionally permanent and begins shaping identity, behavior, and perception.

The heart was not created to carry endless resentment.

Healing does not deny what happened. It simply refuses to allow suffering to become the permanent ruler of emotional life. The moment a person chooses peace over bitterness, restoration quietly begins.

Ending Quotes

"Get rid of all bitterness, rage and anger, brawling and slander, along with every form of malice."
— Ephesians 4:31

"A heart at peace gives life to the body, but envy rots the bones."
— Proverbs 14:30
"The bitter heart remembers every wound. The healed heart remembers the lesson without remaining imprisoned by the pain."
— Levi Sap Nei Thang

"Bitterness and jealousy often reinforce one another."
— Levi Sap Nei Thang

Review Questions

1. How does unresolved emotional pain gradually develop into bitterness?
2. Why does bitterness often reshape perception and emotional interpretation over time?
3. How can resentment become emotionally addictive or psychologically familiar?
4. In what ways can bitterness affect relationships, families, and social environments?
5. Why do comparison and envy often strengthen bitterness?
6. What is the difference between healthy grief and long-term bitterness?
7. How does chronic bitterness affect emotional and physical well-being?
8. Why may peace initially feel unfamiliar to deeply bitter individuals?
9. What role do forgiveness, gratitude, and emotional honesty play in healing bitterness?
10. Why is emotional restoration possible even after long periods of resentment?

Chapter 8
The No-Shame Reflex
When Cruelty Becomes Strategy

Opening Quote

"Without discernment, intimidation may be mistaken for confidence, and cruelty may be mistaken for power."
— Levi Sap Nei Thang

In This Chapter

This chapter explores how repeated bitterness, emotional corruption, unresolved shame, or survival-based behavior can gradually erode empathy, remorse, and moral restraint. It examines strategic cruelty, humiliation as power, shameless manipulation, emotional domination, public degradation, emotional sadism, and the psychological process through which cruelty becomes normalized and emotionally efficient. The chapter also discusses why emotionally healthy people are often shocked by shameless individuals and how emotional conscience can become progressively desensitized over time.

Chapter Outline

Opening Reflection

Most emotionally healthy people assume cruelty has limits.

They believe that eventually a person will feel guilty, embarrassed, remorseful, or internally conflicted after humiliating, manipulating, exploiting, or emotionally harming someone else.

But not everyone operates from the same emotional conscience.

Some individuals become so emotionally hardened, bitter, power-driven, or psychologically desensitized that shame itself gradually disappears from behavior. Actions that once would have triggered guilt gradually become normalized. Emotional cruelty stops feeling morally disturbing and instead becomes emotionally useful.

Humiliation becomes strategy.
Manipulation becomes survival.
Mockery becomes entertainment.
Emotional domination becomes power.
The most disturbing part is not always the cruelty itself.
It is the absence of remorse afterward.

This chapter explores how some individuals gradually lose emotional inhibition and begin using cruelty strategically, why emotionally healthy people often struggle to understand this behavior, and how repeated emotional corruption can slowly disconnect people from empathy, accountability, and conscience itself.

Chapter Overview

Human conscience normally creates emotional resistance against harming others unnecessarily. Shame, empathy, guilt, remorse, and emotional discomfort help regulate social behavior and preserve relational trust. These emotional mechanisms discourage cruelty and encourage accountability.

However, under certain psychological conditions, these internal restraints can weaken significantly.

Repeated bitterness, unresolved resentment, emotional survival conditioning, narcissistic entitlement, chronic power-seeking, humiliation-based environments, or prolonged emotional desensitization may gradually erode emotional conscience over time. As empathy weakens, cruelty becomes easier to perform psychologically.

Eventually, some individuals no longer evaluate behavior primarily through moral reflection. Instead, behavior becomes evaluated through usefulness:

- Does it gain control?
- Does it protect status?
- Does it silence opposition?
- Does it create advantage?
- Does it avoid vulnerability?

This chapter examines how shame becomes suppressed, how cruelty transforms into relational strategy, and why emotionally healthy individuals are often deeply disturbed when encountering people who no longer appear internally restrained by guilt or empathy.

Most importantly, this chapter explains that the loss of shame is not emotional strength. It is often evidence of deep emotional corruption or psychological desensitization.

8.1 The Purpose of Healthy Shame

Healthy shame serves an important psychological function.

It helps human beings recognize when behavior violates empathy, morality, dignity, or relational trust. Healthy shame creates emotional discomfort after cruelty, dishonesty, humiliation, exploitation, or betrayal.

Without some degree of shame, social relationships become psychologically unsafe.

Healthy shame says:

"I should not have done that."
"I hurt someone."
"This behavior was wrong."

This emotional discomfort creates accountability and encourages behavioral correction.

However, shame becomes dangerous when it is either excessive or completely absent.

Excessive shame produces self-hatred, emotional paralysis, and chronic insecurity. But absent shame creates a different danger entirely: emotional permission without restraint.

When shame disappears completely, behavior increasingly becomes governed by power, impulse, advantage, or emotional appetite instead of conscience.

8.2 How Cruelty Becomes Normalized

Cruelty rarely becomes strategic overnight.

In many cases, emotional desensitization happens gradually through repetition. At first, the individual may feel discomfort after humiliating or harming others. But if the behavior repeatedly produces:

- control,
- attention,
- emotional release,
- social dominance,
- financial gain,
- or psychological satisfaction,

the conscience may slowly become quieter.

What once felt wrong eventually begins feeling efficient.

A person who repeatedly manipulates others successfully may stop questioning manipulation morally. Someone who repeatedly humiliates vulnerable individuals without consequence may begin viewing cruelty as normal social behavior.

Over time, the emotional barrier weakens.

Cruel behavior becomes easier, faster, and more emotionally automatic because the nervous system no longer experiences strong moral resistance internally.

This is one reason cruelty often escalates progressively.

Behavior that once shocked the conscience eventually stops triggering emotional discomfort altogether.

8.3 Humiliation as Power

Some individuals use humiliation strategically because humiliation creates psychological dominance.

Public embarrassment weakens another person emotionally while elevating the aggressor temporarily. Mockery creates social imbalance. Emotional degradation establishes control by forcing the vulnerable person into shame, defensiveness, or emotional collapse.

For deeply insecure individuals, humiliating others may create temporary emotional superiority.

This explains why some people:

- mock weakness,
- expose vulnerabilities publicly,
- ridicule emotional pain,
- weaponize private information,
- or emotionally degrade others during conflict.

The goal is often not truth.
The goal is emotional positioning.
By making another person appear smaller, the aggressor temporarily feels larger internally.

However, humiliation-based power is psychologically unstable because it depends upon keeping others emotionally beneath the aggressor continuously.

As a result, relationships organized around humiliation eventually become emotionally destructive environments.

8.4 When Empathy Weakens

Empathy allows people to emotionally imagine the pain of others.
It creates hesitation before causing unnecessary harm.

But empathy can weaken under prolonged emotional corruption, chronic bitterness, repeated aggression, narcissistic entitlement, or environments where cruelty becomes normalized socially.

Some individuals gradually stop emotionally registering the humanity of the people they hurt. Others become so consumed by self-interest, resentment, envy, or emotional survival that other people's suffering feels emotionally irrelevant.

This does not always mean the person is incapable of emotion entirely.

Often empathy becomes selective.

They may still feel empathy toward themselves, toward people who benefit them, or toward individuals they identify with personally. But empathy toward vulnerable targets weakens dramatically.

Once empathy decreases, cruelty becomes psychologically easier because the emotional cost internally becomes smaller.

The person no longer fully feels the relational damage they create.

8.5 Strategic Cruelty and Emotional Calculation

Some individuals become highly calculated emotionally.

Instead of reacting impulsively alone, they learn how to use:

- shame,
- fear,
- guilt,
- silence,
- manipulation,
- intimidation,
- emotional withdrawal,
- or humiliation strategically.

Emotional harm becomes increasingly calculated.

The person may carefully identify vulnerabilities in others and exploit them intentionally during conflict. Emotional attacks become designed not merely to express anger but to destabilize, weaken, silence, or control another person psychologically.

Some individuals even study emotional reactions carefully:

- what triggers insecurity,
- what creates guilt,
- what causes emotional collapse,
- or what weakens resistance.

This behavior becomes especially dangerous because it combines emotional detachment with strategic intent.

The person no longer asks:

> "Is this wrong?"

Instead they ask:
"Will this help me win?"

8.6 Why Emotionally Healthy People Become Shocked

Emotionally healthy individuals often struggle to understand shameless cruelty because they unconsciously assume everyone possesses similar emotional restraints internally.

They expect:

- remorse after lying,
- guilt after humiliation,
- empathy after emotional harm,
- or accountability after cruelty.

When those reactions never appear, emotionally healthy individuals become confused and psychologically destabilized.

They may repeatedly ask:
"How could someone do this without guilt?"
"How can they sleep peacefully afterward?"
"Do they not care at all?"

This confusion often keeps vulnerable people trapped longer because they continue waiting for conscience to activate naturally inside the aggressor.

Unfortunately, when emotional desensitization becomes severe, remorse may become extremely limited or strategically performed rather than deeply experienced.

This is why discernment matters.
Not every apology reflects transformation.
Some apologies simply function as emotional damage control.

8.7 The Relationship Between Shame and Sadism

Some emotionally corrupted individuals begin deriving satisfaction from emotional domination itself.

This is where cruelty becomes especially dangerous psychologically.

Emotional sadism occurs when another person's humiliation, fear, collapse, or emotional pain produces gratification, stimulation, amusement, or emotional empowerment.

This often appears through:

- mocking vulnerability,
- provoking emotional breakdowns,
- humiliating others publicly,
- manipulating emotional reactions,
- or enjoying another person's emotional helplessness.

Deep unresolved shame sometimes contributes to this pattern.

A person who secretly feels powerless, inferior, humiliated, or emotionally broken may attempt to reverse these feelings through domination over others.

By controlling another person emotionally, they temporarily escape confronting their own internal emptiness or shame.

But domination never heals shame.
It only spreads suffering outward.

8.8 Environments That Reward Cruelty

Cruelty becomes especially dangerous in environments where it is rewarded socially.

Some families, workplaces, social groups, online spaces, or cultural systems normalize:

- humiliation,
- emotional aggression,
- ridicule,
- public shaming,
- emotional intimidation,
- or manipulation.

In these environments, empathy may be interpreted as weakness while emotional cruelty becomes associated with power, status, intelligence, or social dominance.

Over time, repeated exposure to these systems can desensitize individuals morally.

The person gradually adapts emotionally to survive the environment itself.

This is one reason cruelty sometimes spreads collectively. Individuals begin imitating emotionally destructive behavior because the environment rewards domination more than compassion.

When cruelty becomes normalized socially, conscience often weakens collectively as well.

In digital environments, cruelty may become amplified through attention economies that reward outrage, humiliation, ridicule, and public conflict with visibility and engagement. Over time, repeated exposure to these dynamics can further normalize emotional aggression socially.

8.9 Admiration of Survival-Based Success

In many cases, the individuals who most strongly admire survival-driven, emotionally aggressive, or bitterness-based personalities are often people carrying similar unresolved wounds themselves.

Because they share similar frustrations, insecurities, resentments, humiliation, or survival conditioning, they may interpret emotional hardness, intimidation, manipulation, dominance, or relentless ambition as strength rather than dysfunction.

Without emotional discernment, unhealthy behaviors can easily be mistaken for boldness, fearlessness, confidence, leadership, or the mentality of a "fighter."

For individuals still psychologically trapped in survival thinking, visible financial success, social status, dominance, influence, or public recognition may become proof that the behavior is justified, effective, or even admirable.

As a result, some people begin idealizing personalities who appear powerful, wealthy, untouchable, emotionally intimidating, or aggressively successful because they unconsciously wish to escape their own feelings of weakness, poverty, insignificance, humiliation, rejection, or lack of control.

People who come from similar backgrounds of deprivation, instability, emotional hardship, rejection, or social struggle may especially identify with these individuals. The successful survivor may appear fearless, victorious, powerful, or untouchable against a world that once oppressed or ignored them.

In some environments, this admiration becomes socially reinforced:

- Ruthlessness is interpreted as confidence.

- Emotional hardness is mistaken for maturity.
- Manipulation is reframed as intelligence.
- Dominance is celebrated as leadership.
- Aggression is confused with strength.
- Fearlessness without conscience is viewed as power.

Over time, unhealthy behaviors may become normalized because they appear effective.

This creates a dangerous psychological distortion. People no longer evaluate behavior primarily through morality, empathy, accountability, emotional stability, or integrity. Instead, behavior becomes judged mainly through visible outcomes such as wealth, status, influence, popularity, control, or upward mobility.

The admiration often becomes even stronger when the successful individual appears to have escaped poverty, humiliation, powerlessness, or social rejection. For some followers, the individual becomes symbolic proof that survival-based behavior "works."

As a result, some people begin aspiring not only toward the success itself, but also toward the emotionally unhealthy behaviors associated with achieving it.

However, visible success does not automatically indicate emotional health, moral integrity, wisdom, or healed character.

Some individuals achieve external success while remaining internally consumed by bitterness, resentment, emotional instability, manipulation, selfishness, narcissistic tendencies, or unresolved trauma.

A society that admires success without discernment may eventually reward destructive behavior simply because it produces visible results.

True success must be measured not only by achievement, but also by integrity, emotional stability, accountability, empathy, and the ability to build healthy relationships without destroying others in the process.

8.10 Survival Thinking and Moral Compromise

In some environments shaped by extreme poverty, instability, corruption, or desperation, survival can become psychologically prioritized above honesty, accountability, or long-term ethical thinking.

Under these conditions, some individuals may begin rationalizing behaviors they would not otherwise consider acceptable. The goal becomes escape, opportunity, financial survival, or social mobility at any cost.

In certain cases, individuals fabricate stories, exaggerate suffering, falsify identities, or manipulate systems in order to obtain immigration opportunities, refugee status, financial assistance, or access to more stable countries. Others may participate in identity fraud, document fraud, or organized schemes designed to bypass legal processes.

Many people who engage in these behaviors justify them internally through survival logic:

"I had no choice."
"Everyone does it."
"This is the only way to escape poverty."
"The system would never help me otherwise."

Many individuals eventually rebuild their lives honorably after reaching safety or opportunity. They work hard, develop stability, and leave survival-based behaviors behind.

However, others remain psychologically trapped in the same mentality even after their circumstances improve.

When deception becomes repeatedly rewarded, dishonesty can become normalized. Manipulation may evolve from a temporary survival tactic into a permanent behavioral pattern. Over time, the person may lose shame surrounding fabrication, exploitation, false accusations, emotional manipulation, or destructive behavior toward others.

In severe cases, individuals who became conditioned to survival-based deception may continue creating false narratives, distorting reality, damaging reputations, manipulating sympathy, or harming innocent people for personal advantage.

This does not occur because poverty automatically creates immoral people. Rather, prolonged survival conditioning can gradually distort ethical boundaries when accountability, healing, and moral self-reflection never develop.

Healthy healing requires more than escaping poverty externally. It also requires rebuilding internal integrity, responsibility, empathy, and moral stability.

In some cases, individuals who become psychologically conditioned to manipulation may continue using past hardship, displacement, or refugee identity as a permanent shield against accountability. Genuine suffering becomes repeatedly used to justify harmful behavior, deflect criticism, gain sympathy, or avoid responsibility for present actions.

Over time, the person may begin weaponizing victimhood itself. Any challenge, disagreement, or accountability is reframed as persecution, cruelty, discrimination, or oppression. Rather than processing past pain in a healthy way, the individual unconsciously converts suffering into social leverage.

This creates a dangerous psychological pattern in which personal history is no longer used for healing, but for control, manipulation, protection from accountability, or emotional domination over others.

Past suffering can explain behavior.

It does not automatically excuse destructive behavior indefinitely.

In some cases, unresolved survival conditioning, chronic resentment, ideological extremism, criminal opportunism, or failure to psychologically adapt to stable social systems may contribute to destructive behavior even after resettlement.

In rare but highly visible cases, a small minority of individuals may engage in riots, vandalism, violence, exploitation of public systems, or antisocial behavior within the very societies that provided them refuge and opportunity. When this occurs, the issue is not refugee status itself, but the continuation of unresolved instability, resentment, lawlessness, or survival-based thinking patterns that were never psychologically addressed.

Healthy integration requires more than physical relocation. It also requires personal accountability, emotional healing, respect for social order, and willingness to adapt constructively to the responsibilities of stable society.

In some cases, individuals who become deeply shaped by resentment, chronic grievance, or survival-based opportunism may eventually begin attacking, undermining, or attempting to destroy the very institutions, systems, relationships, or platforms that once helped elevate, protect, or support them.

Rather than developing gratitude, responsibility, or long-term stability, unresolved bitterness may distort perception. The person begins viewing support systems not as opportunities to build upon, but as structures to exploit, resent, blame, or rebel against once personal expectations are no longer fully satisfied.

This pattern may appear in personal relationships, workplaces, political movements, social systems, or public platforms. Individuals who were once promoted, defended, assisted, or empowered may later become aggressively hostile toward the very environments that enabled their advancement.

Psychologically, this often reflects unresolved internal instability rather than genuine strength. Gratitude, accountability, and emotional maturity were never fully developed alongside external opportunity.

8.11 Healing the Conscience

The loss of shame is not irreversible.
But healing requires emotional honesty and accountability.
The individual must eventually recognize:

> "My behavior is harming people."
> "I have become emotionally desensitized."
> "Cruelty is no longer disturbing me the way it should."

Without this awareness, emotional corruption usually deepens progressively.

Healing the conscience often requires:

- humility,
- accountability,
- empathy restoration,
- spiritual reflection,
- emotional honesty,
- and confronting the pain or shame underneath the cruelty itself.

Many emotionally cruel individuals never learned healthy emotional regulation, empathy, or accountability during formative years. Others became emotionally hardened through bitterness, humiliation, survival conditioning, or repeated exposure to aggression.

But emotional healing remains possible when conscience is no longer suppressed continuously.

"Create in me a clean heart, O God, and renew a right spirit within me."
— Psalm 51:10

The goal of healing is not weakness.
It is restored humanity.

Key Insight

When shame disappears, cruelty becomes emotionally efficient.

A person who no longer feels moral resistance internally may begin using humiliation, manipulation, and emotional harm strategically because conscience no longer interrupts behavior strongly enough.

Summary

This chapter explored how repeated bitterness, emotional corruption, unresolved shame, survival conditioning, and desensitization can gradually erode empathy, guilt, and moral restraint. It examined humiliation as power, strategic cruelty, emotional manipulation, emotional sadism, and why emotionally healthy individuals often become shocked by shameless behavior.

The chapter also discussed how environments can normalize cruelty collectively and emphasized that healing requires restoring conscience, empathy, accountability, and emotional honesty.

Conclusion

Cruelty becomes most dangerous when it no longer feels wrong.

When shame disappears, people may begin treating emotional harm as strategy rather than moral failure. Vulnerability becomes exploitable. Compassion becomes weakness. Human beings become objects to dominate rather than people to protect.

But emotional numbness is not strength.
The absence of guilt is not maturity.

A conscience that no longer reacts to cruelty is not emotionally evolved. It is emotionally damaged.

Healing begins when the heart becomes disturbed by cruelty again.

Ending Reflection

Some of the most dangerous people are not those who explode emotionally in obvious rage. Sometimes the most dangerous individuals are calm, strategic, emotionally detached people who learned how to use cruelty efficiently without visible remorse.

They no longer seek connection.
They seek control.

Yet even deeply hardened individuals were not originally created without conscience. Something slowly numbed empathy, silenced shame, or normalized emotional harm inside them over time.

The tragedy is not only the suffering they create in others.

The deeper tragedy is what repeated cruelty eventually destroys inside the person themselves.

A soul that no longer feels disturbed by unnecessary harm has already lost something deeply human.

Ending Quotes

"Their conscience has been seared as with a hot iron."
— 1 Timothy 4:2

"Whoever conceals hatred with lying lips and spreads slander is a fool."
— Proverbs 10:18

"When cruelty becomes strategy, conscience has already begun to die."
— Levi Sap Nei Thang

"The absence of shame is not freedom. Sometimes it is evidence of emotional decay."
— Levi Sap Nei Thang

"A healthy soul feels disturbed after causing unnecessary pain."
— Levi Sap Nei Thang

"Without discernment, intimidation may be mistaken for confidence, and cruelty may be mistaken for power."
— Levi Sap Nei Thang

Review Questions

1. What psychological purpose does healthy shame serve?
2. How does cruelty gradually become normalized?
3. Why do some individuals use humiliation strategically?
4. How does weakened empathy contribute to emotional cruelty?
5. What is strategic cruelty?
6. Why are emotionally healthy people often shocked by shameless individuals?
7. What role does unresolved shame play underneath domination and cruelty?
8. How can environments normalize emotional aggression collectively?
9. What does healing the conscience require?

Chapter 9
The Shadow Wound

Why Bitter People Attack the Vulnerable

Opening Quote

"The tongue has the power of life and death."
— Proverbs 18:21

In This Chapter

This chapter explores why emotionally bitter individuals sometimes target emotionally vulnerable, peaceful, compassionate, or emotionally stable people. It examines projection, emotional displacement, envy, resentment toward innocence or peace, and the psychological dynamics behind verbal aggression, emotional sabotage, and relational hostility. The chapter also discusses emotional predation, insecurity, shame, and how vulnerable individuals can protect themselves without becoming emotionally hardened.

Chapter Outline

Opening Reflection
Chapter Overview
9.1 When Pain Searches for a Target
9.2 Why Peaceful People Sometimes Trigger Bitter Individuals
9.3 Projection: Fighting Internal Pain Through Other People
9.4 Emotional Predators and Safe Targets
9.5 The Relationship Between Shame and Aggression
9.6 Why Vulnerable People Often Stay Too Long
9.7 Protecting Softness Without Losing It
9.8 Not Every Bitter Person Is Evil
9.9 Healing the Cycle
Key Insight
Summary
Conclusion
Ending Reflection
Ending Quotes
Review Questions

Opening Reflection

Not every attack begins with hatred.

Sometimes people attack others because they are internally at war with themselves.

A bitter heart often struggles to tolerate peace in others. Calmness, kindness, innocence, emotional stability, or vulnerability may unintentionally trigger unresolved emotions inside deeply wounded individuals. Instead of confronting their own pain directly, they redirect emotional frustration outward toward safer targets.

The vulnerable often become those targets.

Gentle people are frequently mistaken for weak people. Compassion is mistaken for inability to defend oneself. Emotional softness is interpreted as an opportunity for domination, manipulation, ridicule, or emotional control.

But many attacks against vulnerable individuals are not actually about the vulnerable person at all. They are reflections of unresolved pain, insecurity, resentment, shame, or emotional instability within the aggressor.

This chapter explores why emotionally bitter individuals sometimes attack those who appear emotionally safer, softer, or more peaceful than themselves, and why understanding this dynamic is important for emotional protection and healing.

Chapter Overview

Throughout human relationships, emotionally wounded individuals sometimes redirect unresolved pain toward vulnerable people rather than toward the true source of their suffering. This process is psychologically complex and often unconscious.

Some bitter individuals feel emotionally threatened by kindness because kindness exposes the emotional harshness they carry internally. Others resent emotional innocence because it reminds them of qualities they believe they lost through suffering. In some cases, emotionally vulnerable individuals are targeted simply because they appear less likely to retaliate.

This chapter examines emotional displacement, projection, resentment toward emotional peace, and the psychological mechanisms through which bitterness becomes relational aggression. It also explores how emotional predators identify vulnerable targets and why emotionally healthy boundaries are essential for protection.

Most importantly, this chapter emphasizes that vulnerability itself is not weakness. Emotional gentleness becomes dangerous only when it exists without discernment, boundaries, or self-protection.

9.1 When Pain Searches for a Target

Many emotionally bitter individuals carry unresolved anger that never found healthy resolution. Instead of processing pain internally, they unconsciously search for external targets onto whom emotional frustration can be discharged.

This process is often called emotional displacement.

The original source of pain may have been:

- rejection,
- humiliation,
- abandonment,
- abuse,
- failure,
- shame,
- betrayal,
- or chronic emotional neglect.

However, confronting the true source directly may feel emotionally unsafe, impossible, or psychologically overwhelming. As a result, the unresolved emotional tension seeks release elsewhere.

The vulnerable often become easier targets because they appear emotionally safer to attack.

A peaceful individual may be criticized harshly. A gentle person may be mocked. Someone emotionally soft-spoken may become the object of verbal aggression because the bitter person unconsciously assumes there will be little resistance.

In many situations, the attack is less about hatred and more about emotional discharge.

The aggressor temporarily relieves internal tension by transferring pain outward.

9.2 Why Peaceful People Sometimes Trigger Bitter Individuals

Emotionally bitter people are often deeply uncomfortable around genuine emotional peace.

A calm, emotionally grounded, compassionate person may unintentionally expose the internal chaos the bitter individual carries inside. This contrast can create psychological discomfort.

Instead of inspiring healing, the peaceful person may trigger resentment.

The bitter individual may begin criticizing:

- kindness as weakness,
- gentleness as naïveté,
- emotional stability as fake,
- or compassion as manipulation.

In reality, these reactions often reveal internal insecurity rather than objective truth.

Sometimes emotionally wounded individuals resent people who still possess emotional qualities they themselves feel they lost. Innocence, hope, warmth, emotional openness, and trust may remind them of earlier versions of themselves before pain transformed their emotional world.

This can produce unconscious hostility toward emotionally softer individuals.

Rather than grieving their own emotional losses directly, some individuals attack the qualities they can no longer comfortably tolerate seeing in others.

9.3 Projection: Fighting Internal Pain Through Other People

Projection occurs when individuals unconsciously place their own emotions, insecurities, or unresolved conflicts onto others.

A deeply insecure person may constantly accuse others of weakness. A dishonest person may become highly suspicious of everyone else. A person carrying shame may aggressively expose or criticize others to avoid confronting their own internal discomfort.

Bitterness frequently operates through projection.

The individual may attack vulnerable people not because those people are truly dangerous or defective, but because they psychologically represent emotions the bitter person cannot tolerate within themselves.

For example:

- vulnerability may trigger buried shame,
- kindness may trigger guilt,
- peace may trigger inner emptiness,
- or emotional stability may expose internal instability.

Instead of confronting these painful emotions internally, the bitter person externalizes the conflict onto another human being.

Projection allows temporary psychological relief, but it prevents genuine healing because the true emotional problem remains unresolved internally.

9.4 Emotional Predators and Safe Targets

Some individuals consciously or unconsciously seek emotionally safer targets for domination, humiliation, or emotional control.

Emotionally vulnerable people are often selected because they:

- avoid conflict,
- seek peace,
- desire approval,
- fear rejection,
- struggle with boundaries,
- or possess strong empathy.

Emotional predators frequently test boundaries slowly. The behavior may begin with subtle criticism, sarcasm, emotional manipulation, ridicule, dismissiveness, guilt-inducing behavior, or small acts of disrespect.

Over time, if resistance remains weak, the behavior may escalate.

The vulnerable person often remains confused because emotionally aggressive individuals may alternate between:

- cruelty and kindness,
- criticism and praise,
- affection and hostility,
- apology and repetition.

This inconsistency creates emotional confusion and psychological instability in the target.

Many emotionally vulnerable individuals continue tolerating harmful treatment because they hope the aggressor will eventually change, calm down, or become emotionally healthy.

Unfortunately, unresolved bitterness rarely improves without accountability and self-awareness.

9.5 The Relationship Between Shame and Aggression

Deep shame frequently exists underneath chronic emotional aggression.

Individuals who secretly feel inadequate, rejected, emotionally inferior, or internally damaged sometimes overcompensate through domination, criticism, emotional intimidation, or hostility toward others.

Attacking vulnerable people temporarily creates an illusion of emotional superiority.

For a brief moment, the aggressor feels powerful instead of powerless.

However, this relief is temporary because the original shame remains unresolved internally. As a result, the cycle repeats repeatedly.

This explains why some bitter individuals seem unable to stop criticizing, humiliating, or emotionally attacking others. The behavior is often functioning as a psychological defense against their own internal pain.

Understanding this dynamic does not excuse abusive behavior.

But it helps explain why emotionally wounded individuals sometimes become emotionally dangerous to others.

9.6 Why Vulnerable People Often Stay Too Long

Emotionally vulnerable individuals frequently remain in destructive relationships longer than emotionally healthier individuals.

Several psychological factors contribute to this pattern.

Some vulnerable individuals:

- fear abandonment,
- crave emotional validation,

- confuse suffering with loyalty,
- normalize emotional instability,
- or believe compassion alone can heal another person's bitterness.

Others were raised in emotionally chaotic environments and unconsciously associate instability with familiarity or love.

As a result, they repeatedly tolerate:

- disrespect,
- emotional manipulation,
- verbal cruelty,
- emotional inconsistency,
- or psychological exhaustion.

Many hope that if they remain patient enough, loving enough, forgiving enough, or understanding enough, the bitter individual will eventually transform.

While compassion is valuable, compassion without boundaries often becomes self-destruction.

Love cannot heal someone who refuses responsibility for their own emotional condition.

9.7 Protecting Softness Without Losing It

One of the greatest emotional challenges is learning how to protect emotional softness without becoming emotionally hardened.

Many vulnerable individuals respond to repeated attacks by shutting down emotionally completely. They stop trusting, stop opening emotionally, and gradually become defensive or emotionally numb.

But healing does not require becoming cold.
Healthy emotional protection involves:

- discernment,
- boundaries,
- emotional awareness,
- recognizing manipulation,
- limiting access to destructive individuals,
- and protecting emotional peace.

A soft heart does not need to become a defenseless heart.

Boundaries do not make compassion less pure; they make compassion sustainable.

Emotionally healthy individuals learn how to remain compassionate while also recognizing danger signs earlier. They no longer interpret constant suffering as proof of love or emotional maturity.

Wisdom allows softness to survive safely.

9.8 Not Every Bitter Person Is Evil

It is important to recognize that many bitter individuals are deeply wounded individuals rather than purely malicious people.

Some experienced severe emotional neglect, abuse, humiliation, betrayal, or prolonged instability that gradually reshaped their emotional world. Others never learned healthy emotional regulation, accountability, or secure attachment.

Pain distorted their relational behavior over time.

However, understanding someone's pain does not require tolerating emotional destruction from them indefinitely.

Compassion and boundaries must coexist.

A person may understand the emotional origins of someone's bitterness while still recognizing that the relationship is psychologically unsafe.

Healing requires accountability. Without accountability, bitterness often continues harming others repeatedly.

9.9 Healing the Cycle

The cycle of bitterness and emotional aggression can be interrupted.

But healing begins only when individuals become willing to confront their own pain honestly rather than continuously transferring it onto others.

The bitter individual must eventually recognize:

> "My pain is now hurting other people."

Without this awareness, emotional aggression usually continues repeating itself across relationships and environments.

Likewise, emotionally vulnerable individuals must recognize:

"My softness does not require self-destruction."

Healing for vulnerable people often involves strengthening boundaries, increasing discernment, rebuilding self-worth, and learning that emotional protection is not cruelty.

The goal is not emotional hardness.
The goal is emotionally wise softness.

A healed person remains compassionate without remaining unprotected.

Key Insight

Many attacks against vulnerable individuals are not truly about the vulnerable person.

They are often displaced expressions of unresolved shame, bitterness, insecurity, resentment, or emotional instability within the aggressor.

Understanding this helps vulnerable individuals stop internalizing every attack as proof of their own worthlessness.

Summary

This chapter explored why emotionally bitter individuals sometimes target vulnerable, peaceful, compassionate, or emotionally soft people. It examined emotional displacement, projection, insecurity, shame, emotional predation, and resentment toward emotional peace and innocence.

The chapter also discussed why vulnerable individuals often remain in destructive relational patterns and emphasized the importance of boundaries, discernment, and emotional protection. Ultimately, healing involves preserving compassion while refusing to remain emotionally defenseless against destructive behavior.

Conclusion

A bitter person does not always attack because the vulnerable are weak.

Sometimes they attack because vulnerability exposes the emotional pain they cannot escape within themselves.

Unresolved bitterness often searches for emotionally safer targets through criticism, manipulation, humiliation, or emotional domination. But pain transferred onto others never truly heals the original wound.

Likewise, vulnerable individuals must learn that kindness without boundaries invites repeated harm.

Healing does not require losing softness.

It requires strengthening softness with wisdom, discernment, and self-protection.

Ending Reflection

Some of the kindest people carry the deepest scars because they remained open-hearted in environments that repeatedly wounded them. Over time, many begin believing they must choose between kindness and survival.

But emotional healing is not about choosing hardness over compassion.
It is about learning that gentleness and wisdom must walk together.

A soft heart becomes dangerous only when it lacks boundaries. A wounded heart becomes dangerous when it refuses healing.

The goal is not to become emotionally untouchable.
The goal is to remain human without remaining unprotected.

Ending Quotes

"Be wise as serpents and innocent as doves."
— Matthew 10:16

"Above all else, guard your heart, for everything you do flows from it."
— Proverbs 4:23

"Bitterness attacks softness because softness reminds the bitter heart of what it lost."
— Levi Sap Nei Thang

"Compassion without wisdom becomes vulnerability to destruction."
— Levi Sap Nei Thang

Review Questions

1. What is emotional displacement, and how does it relate to bitterness?
2. Why might peaceful or compassionate individuals trigger resentment in bitter people?
3. How does projection influence emotionally aggressive behavior?
4. Why are emotionally vulnerable individuals often targeted by emotional predators?
5. What role does shame play underneath emotional aggression?
6. Why do vulnerable individuals sometimes remain in destructive relationships too long?
7. How can a person remain emotionally soft without becoming defenseless?
8. Why is understanding someone's pain different from tolerating harmful behavior?
9. What is the difference between emotional hardness and emotionally wise softness?

Chapter 10
The Graveyard of Relationships
Why Every Helper Becomes the Next Enemy

Opening Quote

"Unhealed pain turns relationships into battlegrounds instead of places of peace."
— Levi Sap Nei Thang

In This Chapter

This chapter explores why some emotionally wounded or chronically bitter individuals repeatedly destroy relationships with the very people who tried to help them. It examines emotional instability, projection, resentment, dependency, distrust, self-sabotage, emotional cycling, and the psychological pattern in which helpers eventually become perceived enemies. The chapter also discusses emotional exhaustion among caregivers and why healthy relationships cannot survive without accountability, stability, and emotional responsibility.

Chapter Outline

Opening Reflection

Some people are surrounded by broken relationships everywhere they go.

Former friends become enemies. Supporters become betrayers. Helpers become targets of anger. Relationships begin intensely, emotionally, and hopefully, yet somehow collapse repeatedly into conflict, resentment, exhaustion, or emotional destruction.

At first, it may appear that the person is simply unlucky or constantly surrounded by bad people. But over time, a painful pattern becomes visible:

Every person who gets close eventually becomes the next disappointment.

This cycle is emotionally devastating not only for the wounded individual, but also for those who genuinely tried to care, help, support, rescue, protect, or remain loyal. Many helpers enter the relationship believing compassion, patience, loyalty, or sacrifice will eventually stabilize the situation. Instead, they slowly become emotionally depleted themselves.

This chapter explores why some emotionally unstable or deeply bitter individuals repeatedly turn against the very people who once supported them, and why unresolved pain often transforms relationships into emotional battlegrounds instead of places of safety and healing.

Chapter Overview

Human relationships require emotional trust, accountability, consistency, and psychological safety to remain healthy over time. However, deeply wounded individuals sometimes carry unresolved emotional instability into every relationship they enter.

As a result, relationships begin under intense emotional dependency, idealization, urgency, or attachment, but gradually deteriorate into suspicion, resentment, emotional volatility, blame, or emotional exhaustion.

Many emotionally unstable individuals unconsciously recreate cycles of abandonment and betrayal because instability itself has become emotionally familiar. Helpers initially appear comforting and emotionally safe, but once disappointment, correction, boundaries, or unmet expectations emerge, the helper may suddenly become reclassified emotionally as an enemy.

This chapter examines why emotional instability often produces relational destruction, how unresolved trauma reshapes attachment patterns, and why emotionally healthy people eventually become exhausted when relationships revolve entirely around rescuing, regulating, or surviving another person's emotional chaos.

Most importantly, this chapter explains that compassion alone cannot sustain relationships without emotional responsibility, accountability, and a willingness to heal.

1.1 The Idealization Phase — "You Are the One Who Finally Understands Me"

Many emotionally unstable relationships begin intensely.

At the beginning, the helper may feel unusually valued, trusted, admired, or emotionally needed. The wounded individual may describe the helper as:

- the only person who understands them,
- the only safe person in their life,
- or the only one who has ever truly cared.

This stage often feels emotionally meaningful and deeply bonding.

The helper may feel honored by the trust and emotionally motivated to protect, rescue, comfort, or stabilize the struggling individual. Compassion naturally increases because the wounded person appears emotionally fragile, misunderstood, abandoned, or deeply hurt.

However, the relationship sometimes becomes emotionally dangerous when emotional dependency replaces emotional stability.

Instead of developing healthy attachment gradually, the wounded individual may attach intensely and prematurely, placing unrealistic emotional expectations onto the helper. The helper unconsciously becomes assigned responsibility for emotional regulation, emotional safety, emotional validation, and psychological stability.

At first, this may appear loving.
Over time, it often becomes emotionally unsustainable.

10.2 When Disappointment Becomes Betrayal

Healthy relationships tolerate imperfection.
Emotionally unstable relationships often do not.

In emotionally unstable dynamics, even small disappointments may become emotionally magnified into feelings of abandonment, rejection, humiliation, or betrayal. A delayed response, emotional boundary, disagreement, correction, or unmet expectation may trigger disproportionately intense emotional reactions.

The helper who was once idealized suddenly becomes emotionally dangerous in the mind of the wounded individual.

This shift is psychologically important.

The relationship may move rapidly from:

- admiration to resentment,
- closeness to hostility,
- dependence to accusation,
- or emotional attachment to emotional warfare.

This often occurs because unresolved emotional wounds from the past are being unconsciously projected onto present relationships.

The current helper is no longer being seen clearly as an individual person. Instead, they become emotionally fused with previous disappointments, betrayals, or abandonment experiences stored inside the wounded person's emotional memory.

As a result, ordinary relational tension becomes psychologically experienced as catastrophic rejection.

10.3 Why Helpers Eventually Become Enemies

Many helpers eventually become targets of anger because helpers occupy emotionally vulnerable positions.

The helper often sees:

- emotional weakness,
- emotional dependency,

- instability,
- shame,
- fear,
- insecurity,
- or psychological fragility.

Over time, this exposure itself may begin triggering discomfort inside the wounded individual.

Some emotionally unstable individuals eventually resent the very people who witnessed their vulnerability. Others feel ashamed of their dependency and unconsciously convert shame into hostility.

Instead of feeling grateful, they begin feeling emotionally exposed.

The helper becomes psychologically associated with:

- weakness,
- helplessness,
- emotional need,
- or moments of emotional collapse.

This creates internal discomfort that may later transform into criticism, blame, distancing, emotional attacks, or resentment.

Ironically, the more the helper sacrificed emotionally, the more emotionally dangerous they may eventually feel to the wounded person because the relationship contains evidence of dependency the individual wishes to escape psychologically.

10.4 Emotional Cycling and Relational Instability

Some individuals repeatedly cycle between emotional closeness and emotional destruction.

The relationship pattern often looks like this:

- Intense attachment
- Emotional dependency
- Fear of abandonment
- Emotional volatility
- Conflict or accusation
- Emotional rupture
- Regret or reconciliation
- Repetition of the cycle

This pattern creates severe emotional exhaustion for everyone involved.

Helpers often become psychologically trapped because the relationship alternates unpredictably between affection and emotional hostility. During peaceful periods, the wounded individual may appear deeply loving, remorseful, emotionally insightful, or emotionally dependent again.

This intermittent emotional reinforcement makes it difficult for helpers to leave.

They continue hoping stability will eventually return permanently.

However, without emotional accountability and healing, the cycle often repeats indefinitely.

Emotional intensity should never be confused with emotional health.

10.5 Psychological Attachment to Status and Stability

In some cases, unresolved survival conditioning may lead individuals to pursue relationships primarily for access to status, visibility, financial opportunity, influence, or social elevation. Successful, stable, or publicly respected individuals may gradually be viewed less as human beings and more as pathways toward personal advancement, validation, or escape from previous insecurity.

Over time, the relationship can become psychologically transactional, where proximity to success is unconsciously used to elevate identity, social standing, credibility, or perceived worth. This dynamic does not represent healthy ambition or normal networking. Rather, it reflects unresolved internal insecurity attempting to stabilize itself through external association.

Because financial insecurity often remains psychologically central within Poverty Bitterness Syndrome, some individuals may become disproportionately focused on relationships that provide access to financial stability, status, influence, opportunity, or upward mobility.

In emotionally unhealthy cases, attachment may form not only from genuine emotional connection, but also from what the relationship symbolically represents psychologically:

- security,
- advancement,
- validation,

- visibility,
- protection, or
- social credibility.

As emotional dependency deepens, the successful or stable individual may gradually become psychologically idealized. The relationship begins carrying emotional weight far beyond normal human connection, increasing the likelihood of disappointment, resentment, instability, or conflict when expectations are no longer fulfilled.

10.6 Resentment Toward the Very People Who Helped

One of the most painful relational patterns within unresolved emotional instability is the gradual development of resentment toward the very people who once provided support, opportunity, compassion, stability, or protection.

At the beginning of the relationship, the helper is often deeply valued. They may be viewed as trustworthy, generous, emotionally safe, financially stable, influential, understanding, or uniquely supportive during a period of struggle. The wounded individual may initially express strong gratitude, admiration, dependency, emotional closeness, or loyalty.

However, over time, unresolved insecurity, shame, bitterness, comparison, dependency, or internal instability can begin distorting the relationship psychologically.

The very presence of a stable or successful person may eventually become emotionally uncomfortable for someone who feels internally inadequate, powerless, resentful, or left behind. Instead of inspiring healing, the comparison may silently intensify insecurity.

In some cases, the helper unintentionally becomes a living reminder of everything the wounded individual feels they lack:

stability, recognition, success, emotional control, opportunity, peace, financial security, healthy relationships, or social respect.

As this internal tension grows, appreciation may slowly transform into resentment.

The person who once represented safety may eventually become perceived as controlling, selfish, arrogant, disappointing, unfair, emotionally distant, privileged, or exploitative—even when no intentional harm occurred.

In psychologically unstable dynamics, emotional dependency and resentment often begin coexisting simultaneously.

The individual may continue seeking support, attention, access, validation, money, emotional reassurance, influence, or opportunity from the same person they increasingly resent internally.

This creates emotional contradiction:

- they need the relationship,
- but simultaneously resent needing it.

Over time, unresolved bitterness may lead to criticism, manipulation, emotional attacks, betrayal, dishonesty, blame-shifting, public humiliation, passive-aggressive behavior, exploitation, or repeated conflict directed toward the very person who tried to help them.

In some cases, successful, respected, stable, or influential individuals may unconsciously become targets for psychological elevation. Association with them temporarily provides identity reinforcement, validation, social credibility, financial access, opportunity, or perceived advancement.

The relationship gradually becomes less about genuine emotional connection and more about what proximity to the other person psychologically provides.

When expectations are not continually fulfilled, admiration can rapidly collapse into resentment.

This pattern helps explain why some helpers eventually become emotional enemies in deeply unstable relationships.

The tragedy is that many helpers continue trying harder, believing more sacrifice, patience, money, understanding, reassurance, or compassion will eventually repair the instability.

But unresolved emotional wounds cannot be permanently stabilized through external support alone.

Without accountability, healing, emotional regulation, gratitude, and personal responsibility, the cycle often repeats regardless of how much help is given.

Healthy relationships cannot survive when appreciation continually transforms into resentment and support repeatedly becomes a source of emotional hostility.

10.7 Projection and the Fear of Being Abandoned

Many emotionally unstable individuals carry profound fear of abandonment.

Ironically, this fear sometimes produces the very behaviors that eventually push people away.

The wounded individual may become:

- suspicious,
- controlling,
- emotionally reactive,
- accusatory,
- demanding,
- or emotionally overwhelming.

As tension increases, relationships weaken. Eventually, the helper becomes emotionally exhausted or begins creating healthy boundaries.

The wounded person then interprets this withdrawal as confirmation of abandonment fears:

> "Everyone eventually leaves me."

What remains unseen is how unresolved emotional instability contributed to the relational collapse itself.

This process often involves projection.

Past abandonment wounds become projected onto present relationships until every relational disappointment feels like proof that abandonment is inevitable.

Without healing, the person unknowingly recreates the emotional conditions they fear most.

10.8 The Emotional Exhaustion of Helpers

People who repeatedly help emotionally unstable individuals often experience severe emotional exhaustion themselves.

At first, the helper may feel compassionate, patient, loyal, or emotionally committed to saving the relationship. Over time, however, constant emotional instability produces:

- psychological fatigue,
- anxiety,
- hypervigilance,

- emotional burnout,
- guilt,
- confusion,
- and emotional depletion.

Many helpers slowly lose their own emotional stability while trying to stabilize someone else continuously.

Some begin walking on eggshells emotionally, constantly monitoring their words, tone, reactions, or boundaries to avoid triggering emotional explosions.

Others become trapped in chronic guilt because they feel responsible for the wounded person's emotional survival.

This dynamic becomes psychologically dangerous when the helper sacrifices their own emotional health entirely in order to sustain the relationship.

Compassion without boundaries eventually becomes emotional self-erasure.

Some helpers eventually develop symptoms similar to chronic stress responses because their nervous systems remain continuously activated by unpredictability and emotional instability.

10.9 The Hidden Damage to Victims

One of the most damaging aspects of unresolved survival-based behavior is that the emotional wounds rarely remain isolated within the individual. Over time, the bitterness, instability, manipulation, emotional defensiveness, selfishness, or survival-driven behaviors often spread outward into relationships, leaving emotional damage in the lives of others.

Many victims initially enter these relationships with empathy, patience, compassion, loyalty, or a genuine desire to help. Because emotionally wounded individuals may appear vulnerable, misunderstood, strong, ambitious, charismatic, or emotionally intense, others may feel emotionally drawn toward them before recognizing the deeper instability underneath the surface.

Over time, however, repeated exposure to emotional volatility, manipulation, selfishness, intimidation, dishonesty, emotional inconsistency, blame-shifting, control, or relational instability can begin affecting the victim psychologically and emotionally.

Some victims gradually develop:

- chronic anxiety,
- emotional exhaustion,
- confusion,
- hypervigilance,
- fear of conflict,
- self-doubt,
- guilt,
- lowered self-esteem,
- emotional dependency,
- loss of peace,
- emotional numbness,
- or difficulty trusting others.

Many begin constantly monitoring moods, avoiding disagreement, suppressing their own needs, or walking on eggshells in order to prevent emotional escalation or relational collapse.

In some cases, victims become psychologically trapped in cycles of hope, disappointment, reconciliation, emotional attachment, and repeated hurt. The instability itself may create emotional confusion, especially when moments of affection, validation, success, charm, vulnerability, or temporary kindness are mixed with emotional harm.

Soft-hearted individuals are often especially vulnerable because they naturally try to understand suffering, forgive pain, and see potential for healing in others. Unfortunately, compassion without discernment can sometimes lead individuals to tolerate emotionally destructive patterns far longer than is healthy.

Over time, some victims begin losing their own emotional identity. Their energy becomes consumed by emotional management, survival, repairing conflict, avoiding tension, or trying to stabilize the relationship.

One of the greatest dangers is that emotionally unhealthy environments can slowly normalize dysfunction. Victims may eventually begin accepting manipulation, disrespect, emotional cruelty, instability, selfishness, or emotional exhaustion as "normal" simply because they have experienced it repeatedly for so long.

Not every emotionally wounded individual intentionally harms others. Many people struggle internally while still trying to love, heal, and act responsibly.

However, unresolved pain that is never acknowledged, healed, or controlled can eventually spread suffering into the lives of those closest to the individual.

Healing requires not only compassion for wounded people, but also wisdom, boundaries, accountability, emotional discernment, and the recognition that protecting one's emotional well-being is not selfishness. It is part of emotional responsibility and long-term psychological health.

10.10 Why Accountability Is Necessary for Love

Love alone cannot heal chronic emotional instability.

Compassion matters deeply, but relationships cannot survive long-term without accountability, self-awareness, emotional regulation, and personal responsibility.

Some emotionally wounded individuals expect endless understanding while resisting correction, boundaries, or responsibility for harmful behavior. Over time, this creates profoundly unequal relationships where one person absorbs emotional damage while the other avoids accountability.

Healthy love requires mutual responsibility.

Without accountability:

- apologies lose meaning,
- promises repeat without change,
- emotional harm continues,
- and relational trust slowly dies.

Healing begins only when individuals stop blaming every failed relationship entirely on others and begin examining the emotional patterns they themselves carry into relationships repeatedly.

10.11 The Graveyard Effect

— When Every Relationship Ends the Same Way

Some individuals eventually accumulate what can be called a "graveyard of relationships."

Former friends, partners, helpers, supporters, mentors, caregivers, and family members become emotionally distant or permanently disconnected over time.

The painful pattern is not merely that relationships ended.

It is that they ended similarly.

The names change.
The environments change.
The circumstances change.
Yet the emotional outcome remains strangely repetitive:

- conflict,
- betrayal accusations,
- emotional collapse,
- resentment,
- emotional exhaustion,
- or permanent relational rupture.

When this pattern repeats across many relationships, the problem usually extends beyond isolated bad luck.

Unresolved emotional wounds are often silently recreating relational destruction repeatedly.

This realization can feel painful because it forces the individual to confront the possibility that their unresolved pain is now participating in the collapse of their own relationships.

But this awareness is also where healing begins.

10.12 Healing Relational Destruction

Relational healing requires emotional honesty.

The wounded individual must eventually ask:

"Why do my relationships keep collapsing?"
"Why do people eventually become exhausted around me?"
"Am I repeatedly recreating emotional instability?"

These questions are painful but necessary.

Healing involves learning:

- emotional regulation,
- accountability,
- stable communication,
- boundary respect,
- conflict management,

- and emotional self-awareness.

Likewise, helpers must learn that rescuing another person endlessly is not the same as healing them.

A relationship cannot become healthy if one person carries all emotional responsibility while the other refuses transformation.

Healing relationships requires both compassion and accountability.

Without both, the cycle usually continues.

Key Insight

When unresolved emotional wounds remain unhealed, relationships often become emotional reenactments of past pain rather than places of mutual stability, safety, and growth.

Helpers eventually become enemies because emotional dependency, projection, shame, resentment, and fear distort the relationship itself.

Summary

This chapter explored why emotionally unstable or deeply bitter individuals sometimes repeatedly destroy relationships with the very people who tried to help them. It examined emotional dependency, projection, fear of abandonment, relational cycling, shame, emotional exhaustion among helpers, and the role of accountability in sustaining healthy relationships.

The chapter also discussed the repetitive "graveyard" pattern in which relational destruction continues across many environments and emphasized that healing requires emotional honesty, responsibility, and willingness to confront unresolved pain.

Conclusion

Some people are not surrounded by enemies because everyone betrayed them.

Sometimes unresolved emotional instability transforms every close relationship into a future battlefield.

Without healing, helpers eventually become associated with disappointment, shame, vulnerability, unmet expectations, or emotional exposure. What began as comfort slowly transforms into resentment and emotional conflict.

But this cycle is not irreversible.

Relationships can heal when emotional accountability replaces blame, when self-awareness replaces projection, and when wounded individuals stop demanding rescue while refusing transformation.

A healthy relationship cannot survive on compassion alone.
It also requires responsibility.

Ending Reflection

Many helpers enter wounded relationships believing love will be enough to save another person from their pain. Sometimes compassion does help people heal. But compassion cannot replace accountability, emotional regulation, or personal responsibility.

No relationship survives indefinitely when one person is always rescuing while the other is always collapsing.

Likewise, deeply wounded individuals often do not realize how unresolved pain quietly reshapes every relationship they touch. The fear of abandonment slowly creates the very instability that eventually drives others away.

Healing begins when people stop asking:

> "Why does everyone leave me?"

and begin asking:

> "What pain am I carrying into every relationship?"

That question is painful.
But it is also the beginning of emotional freedom.

Ending Quotes

"Faithful are the wounds of a friend; profuse are the kisses of an enemy."
— Proverbs 27:6

"Do not cast me away when I am old; do not forsake me when my strength is gone."
— Psalm 71:9

"When every helper becomes the next enemy, the wound is no longer only in the past. It has entered the relationship itself."
— Levi Sap Nei Thang

"Compassion can support healing, but it cannot substitute for responsibility."
— Levi Sap Nei Thang

Review Questions

1. Why do some emotionally unstable relationships begin with intense attachment?
2. How can small disappointments become emotionally experienced as betrayal?
3. Why do helpers sometimes become targets of resentment or hostility?
4. What is emotional cycling, and how does it affect relationships?
5. How does fear of abandonment contribute to relational instability?
6. What emotional effects do helpers often experience over time?
7. Why is accountability necessary for healthy love?
8. What is the "graveyard of relationships" pattern?
9. How does emotional honesty contribute to relational healing?

PART III

Healing And Awakening

Chapter 11
Healing the Pattern
Breaking the Cycle from Within

Opening Quote

"Not every relationship can be repaired, but every wounded heart can still pursue healing."
— Levi Sap Nei Thang

In This Chapter

This chapter explores how lasting behavioral change occurs through awareness, accountability, emotional regulation, and intentional interruption of survival-based responses. It examines the process of healing unresolved conditioning, rebuilding relational stability, and learning repair after repeated cycles of conflict and defensiveness. Readers will learn how survival patterns can gradually be transformed into healthier structures grounded in reflection, consistency, responsibility, and emotional stability.

Chapter Outline

Chapter Overview

Understanding a pattern is not the same as changing it.
Recognition brings clarity.
Change requires a decision.

Throughout this book, we have examined how survival-based behavior can continue long after the environment has changed—how conflict becomes necessary, how accountability is redirected, and how stability is repeatedly disrupted.

But patterns do not end on their own.
They continue until something interrupts them.

This chapter examines how that interruption happens—not from the outside, but from within.

11.1 The Condition for Change

No meaningful change can occur without recognition.

External advice, support, or even consequences cannot create lasting transformation on their own. At most, they create a temporary adjustment. Without internal acknowledgment, the underlying pattern remains unchanged.

Change begins when the individual recognizes that their actions have had a real impact—not only on situations, but on people, relationships, and opportunities.

This recognition is not about blame.
It is about ownership.

Until there is a willingness to see the pattern clearly and accept responsibility for its effects, the system continues operating as it always has.

Awareness alone is not enough.

It must be followed by sustained willingness:

- willingness to pause,
- willingness to reflect,
- willingness to change repeated responses.

Without that willingness, no amount of external effort can produce lasting stability.

But when recognition and willingness align, change becomes possible.

11.2 Understanding Healing, Repair, Awareness, and Emotional Regulation

Healing is the gradual process of recognizing, understanding, and changing patterns that no longer support stability, emotional health, or healthy relationships. Healing does not erase past experiences, but it changes how they influence present behavior.

"Create in me a clean heart, O God, and renew a right spirit within me."
— Psalm 51:10

Repair is the process of restoring trust or stability after conflict through acknowledgment, accountability, adjustment, and consistent behavioral change. Repair allows relationships and systems to recover rather than remain trapped in repeated tension.

Awareness is the ability to observe one's own thoughts, behaviors, emotional responses, and patterns with clarity rather than automatic reaction. Awareness creates the possibility for intentional change.

Emotional regulation is the ability to experience emotion without becoming fully controlled by it. It involves recognizing emotional responses, managing intensity, and responding in ways that maintain stability rather than escalation.

"A person without self-control is like a city with broken-down walls."
— Proverbs 25:28

11.3 From Survival to Awareness

The behaviors described in this book did not form randomly.

They were shaped by environments where:

- stability was uncertain,
- resources were limited,

- emotional support was inconsistent.

In those conditions, intensity, control, and rapid response were necessary.
They were not flaws.
They were survival.
The challenge is not their existence.
It is their continuation.

Healing begins when survival shifts into awareness—when responses are no longer automatic, but intentional.

I once observed a young child who had grown up in an orphanage before being adopted into a stable home environment. When she first arrived, she reacted aggressively toward almost anyone who approached her. She scratched, fought over food, guarded possessions intensely, and responded defensively even during harmless interactions.

Her behavior initially appeared hostile and emotionally extreme. However, over time it became clear that these reactions were rooted in survival rather than cruelty. She had learned through repeated experience that safety was uncertain, resources were limited, and vulnerability could lead to harm. Fighting had become part of her nervous system's protection strategy.

What was remarkable was not the severity of the behavior, but the gradual transformation that followed.

After several years in a stable, safe, and emotionally consistent environment, the child slowly changed. The aggression decreased. Trust developed gradually. Emotional softness began returning. Eventually, she became noticeably calmer, gentler, and emotionally safer in relationships.

This illustrates an important reality about survival conditioning: behaviors formed in instability are not always permanent traits. Sometimes they are adaptive responses created by environments where protection felt necessary.

However, healing often requires something many individuals never consistently receive — long-term emotional safety, stability, patience, and healthy relational modeling.

Children sometimes heal more visibly because their emotional systems are still developing. Adults who remain trapped in survival conditioning for decades may find these patterns far more difficult to interrupt because the behaviors have become deeply integrated into identity, relationships, and emotional regulation itself.

11.4 Recognizing the Pattern Without Defending It

One of the most difficult steps is seeing the pattern without immediately justifying it.

Each reaction may feel correct.
Each response may feel necessary.
But repetition reveals structure.

When the same conflict appears across different situations, with different people, and leads to similar outcomes, it is no longer situational.

It is structural.
The question changes from:

"Who caused this?"

to:

"Why does this keep happening?"

This shift is where change begins.

11.5 Interrupting Automatic Reactions

Survival-based responses are immediate.
They happen before reflection.
To change them, there must be interruption.
This does not require perfection.
It requires a pause.

When tension rises:

- delay response,
- observe the impulse,
- allow space between feeling and action.

Even a brief pause begins changing the system.
You are no longer reacting automatically.
You are choosing.

11.6 Understanding What the Behavior Was Protecting

Behind repeated reactions is protection.
Control may protect against instability.
Anger may protect against vulnerability.

Distance may protect against disappointment.
These responses were formed for a reason.
Ignoring that reason does not remove the pattern.
Understanding it does.

Healing requires asking:
"What was I trying to protect?"

When the protection is understood, the behavior no longer needs to operate in the same way.

11.7 Learning Repair and Facing the Consequences

One of the most critical missing elements in this pattern is repair.
In stable systems, conflict is followed by:

- acknowledgment,
- responsibility,
- adjustment.

Without repair, relationships weaken.
With repair, they strengthen.

Learning to say:
"I reacted too strongly."
"That was not fair."
"I need to correct that."
does not reduce strength.

It demonstrates control.

At first, this may feel unfamiliar.
That is expected.
It was not learned before.
Now it is.

Recognition does not remove consequences.

Patterns repeated over time often leave visible impact on relationships, trust, opportunities, and stability.

As awareness develops, there may be temptation to move forward quickly, focusing only on change. But healing also requires acknowledging what has already occurred.

This does not mean remaining trapped in the past.
It means understanding that change is not only internal.
It must also become visible through consistent external behavior over time.

Trust, once weakened, does not return immediately.
Stability, once disrupted, requires time to rebuild.

Healing includes accepting this process without resistance—not as punishment, but as alignment.

11.8 Relearning Stability and Rebuilding Connection

For someone conditioned by instability, calmness can feel unfamiliar.
Even uncomfortable.
There may be tendency to create tension when things feel too quiet.

This is not intentional.
It is conditioning.

Healing requires remaining in stability without disrupting it.

Not every silence needs to be filled.
Not every difference needs to become conflict.
Not every moment requires intensity.

Stability is not weakness.
It is structure.

"Better a patient person than a warrior, one with self-control than one who takes a city."
— Proverbs 16:32

When emotional expression was limited or inconsistent, connection can feel uncertain.

Closeness may trigger discomfort.
Support may feel unfamiliar.

Healing involves allowing connection without redefining it as threat.
It requires choosing not to turn support into opposition.

Over time, safe and consistent interaction becomes the new reference point.

11.9 Forgiveness, Gratitude, and the Decision to Let Go

One of the most difficult but transformative aspects of healing is learning to release the emotional control that past pain continues exerting over present life.

Many individuals carrying unresolved emotional wounds remain psychologically connected to the people who harmed them through anger, resentment, bitterness, or unresolved grief.

Although the original abuse, neglect, humiliation, or instability may have occurred years earlier, its emotional consequences often continue shaping behavior, relationships, communication patterns, and self-perception long afterward.

Without healing, pain frequently reproduces itself socially. Individuals who were deeply wounded may unintentionally project unresolved anger onto spouses, children, friends, coworkers, or unrelated individuals.

Forgiveness does not mean pretending abuse was acceptable, excusing harmful behavior, abandoning accountability, or allowing continued mistreatment.

Rather, forgiveness represents a conscious decision to stop allowing past injury to dominate present emotional functioning.

In many cases, forgiveness is less about restoring relationship with the offender and more about reclaiming internal peace, emotional stability, and psychological freedom.

Healing often begins when individuals recognize that remaining permanently attached to hatred, revenge, or bitterness prolongs the influence of the original wound.

Letting go creates space for emotional regulation, healthier relationships, clearer identity formation, and long-term psychological recovery.

Forgiveness, therefore, is not weakness.
It is the gradual release of emotional captivity.

"Be kind and compassionate to one another, forgiving each other, just as in Christ God forgave you."
— Ephesians 4:32

"Let all bitterness and wrath and anger and clamor and slander be put away from you."
— Ephesians 4:31

Healing also requires difficult realization:

> "I do not want to continue living this way."

For many people, destructive patterns become so familiar that they feel normal. Conflict feels natural. Intensity feels necessary. Bitterness feels justified.

Over time, the pattern becomes intertwined with identity itself.
This is why healing requires more than information.
It requires willingness.

A person must eventually say:

> "This pattern is hurting my relationships."
> "This way of living is exhausting me."
> "I do not want to keep repeating this cycle."
> "I want emotional peace."
> "I want to become emotionally healthier."

Healing begins when a person stops identifying with the pattern and starts choosing freedom from it.

Healing also becomes possible when a person realizes:

> "This behavior may have been learned, repeated, or inherited — but it is not my permanent identity."

A pattern may influence a life for many years without defining the entire person forever. Emotional conditioning can be interrupted. Survival responses can be relearned. Destructive cycles can lose their control. Recognizing this distinction often becomes one of the most hopeful moments in recovery because it separates the individual from the pattern itself.

Gratitude also becomes powerful interruption to bitterness.

Healing does not begin when life becomes perfect.
It begins when perception is no longer completely controlled by pain.

People trapped in survival-based conditioning often become neurologically trained to scan constantly for danger, unfairness, instability, rejection, or loss.

Over time, the mind may become so focused on what is missing that it loses ability to recognize what remains.

Gratitude interrupts this pattern.

It redirects attention toward:

- relationships that still exist,
- opportunities that remain available,
- strengths developed through hardship,
- moments of peace or stability,
- and evidence that life contains more than pain.

Gratitude does not erase trauma.
It prevents trauma from becoming total identity.

Healing often begins with simple recognitions:

- a safe place to sleep,
- one trustworthy person,
- physical survival,
- another day to rebuild,
- the ability to choose differently,
- and realization that the cycle can stop.

The mind struggles to cultivate deep gratitude and perpetual resentment with equal intensity at the same time.

One eventually weakens the other.

Healing often begins when a person stops asking only:

> "Why was this taken from me?"

and slowly begins asking:

> "What still remains that can help me rebuild?"

Hope often begins the moment survival is no longer viewed as the final destination of identity.

11.10 Choosing Different Outcomes

Patterns continue because they produce familiar outcomes.
Breaking them requires different choices.
Not once. Repeatedly.
Choosing:

- pause over reaction,
- clarity over intensity,

- repair over continuation,
- stability over conflict.

At first, these choices feel unnatural.
Over time, they become the new structure.

"Do not be overcome by evil, but overcome evil with good."
— Romans 12:21

11.11 When Support Is Needed

Not all patterns can be resolved alone.
External support may accelerate clarity.
This may include:

- structured reflection,
- guided behavioral work,
- therapeutic support.

Seeking help is not failure.

It is recognition that change sometimes requires new input, guidance, and emotional structure.

Key Insight

Healing begins when survival-based reactions are no longer automatic. Awareness, accountability, emotional regulation, and consistent behavioral change gradually transform instability into structure and conflict into stability.

Summary

This chapter explored how lasting emotional healing requires more than recognizing destructive patterns. True transformation develops through awareness, accountability, emotional regulation, intentional behavioral interruption, and willingness to confront unresolved pain honestly.

The chapter examined how many survival-based behaviors originally formed as protective responses to instability, emotional neglect, insecurity, conflict, or unsafe environments.

Over time, however, these automatic reactions may continue operating long after the original danger has passed, creating repeated conflict, relational instability, defensiveness, emotional exhaustion, and self-sabotaging cycles.

The chapter also discussed the importance of recognizing patterns without immediately defending them, learning emotional repair after conflict, rebuilding trust gradually, understanding what repeated behaviors were originally protecting, and relearning stability without unconsciously disrupting it. It emphasized that healing requires both internal transformation and visible external consistency over time.

Additionally, the chapter explored forgiveness, gratitude, emotional accountability, boundary awareness, and the realization that survival conditioning is not permanent identity.

Healing becomes possible when individuals stop identifying completely with destructive patterns and begin intentionally choosing emotional stability, responsibility, relational repair, and psychological freedom instead.

Ultimately, healing is not about becoming emotionally perfect.

It is about becoming increasingly aware, regulated, responsible, and free from automatic patterns that once controlled behavior and relationships.

Conclusion

The patterns described in this book are not permanent.
They are persistent—but they can change.

What was once necessary does not need to remain constant.
What was once protective does not need to define everything that follows.

Healing is not the removal of strength.
It is the refinement of it.

What was once used for survival can be redirected toward stability, clarity, and control.

When awareness replaces reaction, and consistency replaces repetition, the cycle no longer sustains itself.

And once the cycle no longer sustains itself, a different direction is no longer theoretical.

It becomes lived.

Ending Reflection

Healing rarely happens all at once.

Most destructive patterns were not formed in a single moment, and they are rarely undone in one either. Emotional conditioning develops through repetition, survival, fear, instability, pain, and environments that taught the nervous system how to protect itself quickly. Over time, these responses can begin feeling automatic, necessary, or even inseparable from identity itself.

But survival is not the same as peace.

Many individuals spend years reacting to old wounds without realizing how strongly the past continues shaping present relationships, emotional reactions, communication patterns, and decisions. What once protected them may eventually begin isolating them, exhausting them, or damaging the very relationships they long to preserve.

Healing begins when awareness interrupts repetition.

It begins when a person becomes willing to pause before reacting, reflect before escalating, and accept responsibility without collapsing into shame. Over time, these small interruptions gradually reshape emotional patterns from within.

The goal of healing is not perfection.

It is increasing stability, honesty, accountability, self-awareness, and emotional freedom over time.

A person may carry scars from the past without remaining controlled by them forever.

The cycle can stop.

And when it does, relationships no longer need to become battlegrounds for unresolved pain. They can finally begin becoming places of safety, growth, trust, repair, and peace.

Ending Quotes

"Do not be overcome by evil, but overcome evil with good."
— Romans 12:21

"Create in me a clean heart, O God, and renew a right spirit within me."
— Psalm 51:10

"Healing begins when awareness becomes stronger than automatic reaction."
— Levi Sap Nei Thang

"Healing begins when survival is no longer treated as identity."
— Levi Sap Nei Thang

"Healing does not erase the past. It changes what the past is allowed to control."
— Levi Sap Nei Thang

"Healing requires both a soft heart and strong boundaries."
— Levi Sap Nei Thang

"Healing often begins when a person stops trying to save everyone at the cost of destroying themselves."
— Levi Sap Nei Thang

"Healing does not erase memory. It changes how pain controls the future."
— Levi Sap Nei Thang

"Emotional healing begins when peace becomes more important than emotional survival."

— Levi Sap Nei Thang

"The goal of healing is not becoming emotionally cold. The goal is learning how to stay emotionally healthy."
— Levi Sap Nei Thang

"A healthy heart does not require denying pain in order to practice forgiveness."
— Levi Sap Nei Thang

"True forgiveness releases hatred without surrendering truth."
— Levi Sap Nei Thang

"A healed heart learns how to remain compassionate without remaining emotionally unprotected."
— Levi Sap Nei Thang

"Some people forgive too little and become bitter. Others forgive without discernment and become repeatedly wounded."
— Levi Sap Nei Thang

"Forgiveness is not permission for continued harm. It is freedom from carrying the harm forever."
— Levi Sap Nei Thang

"The emotionally healthy person learns that forgiveness and discernment must grow together."
— Levi Sap Nei Thang

"What once protected survival may eventually prevent peace."
— Levi Sap Nei Thang

"Emotional freedom begins when the wound no longer controls the direction of life."
— Levi Sap Nei Thang

"Repair becomes possible when accountability becomes stronger than defensiveness."
— Levi Sap Nei Thang

"Stability is not the absence of emotion. It is the ability to remain grounded while experiencing it."
— Levi Sap Nei Thang

"A pattern repeated long enough can feel permanent, but repetition is not destiny."
— Levi Sap Nei Thang

"Healing begins when survival is no longer treated as identity."

— Levi Sap Nei Thang

Reflection Questions

1. Have you noticed any emotional patterns that repeat across multiple relationships or situations in your life?
2. Which emotional reactions in your life may have originally developed as survival responses?
3. Are there moments when you react automatically before fully understanding what you are feeling?
4. What situations tend to trigger defensiveness, anger, withdrawal, or emotional escalation most strongly in you?
5. Have you ever justified a repeated behavior before honestly examining its long-term effects?
6. What emotional pain or fear might your behaviors have been trying to protect?
7. Are there relationships in your life that would benefit from repair, accountability, or healthier communication?
8. Have you ever confused emotional intensity with emotional safety, connection, or love?
9. What boundaries, habits, or choices could help interrupt unhealthy emotional cycles in your life?
10. What does forgiveness mean to you personally, and what emotional weight might you still be carrying?
11. What would healing and emotional stability look like if you stopped defining yourself by old wounds and instead began defining yourself through growth, wisdom, gratitude, accountability, and emotional healing?

Chapter 12
Soft but Shielded
The Soft Heart's Awakening

Opening Quote

"A soft heart is beautiful. A soft heart with wisdom is powerful."
— *Levi Sap Nei Thang*

Opening Reflection

Many soft-hearted people enter life believing that goodness naturally produces goodness in return.

They assume honesty will be met with honesty.
Kindness will inspire kindness.
Patience will soften cruelty.
Loyalty will create loyalty.
Compassion will heal wounded people.

Sometimes these beliefs are beautiful.
Sometimes they become dangerous.

Kindhearted individuals often struggle to imagine that some people may intentionally manipulate, exploit, deceive, humiliate, or emotionally drain others without remorse. Because the soft-hearted person operates from empathy internally, they unconsciously assume empathy exists equally in everyone else.

This assumption leaves many compassionate individuals emotionally unprotected.

Over time, repeated disappointment creates an awakening. The person slowly realizes that kindness without discernment invites emotional danger. Compassion without boundaries attracts manipulation. Emotional openness without wisdom creates vulnerability to emotionally unhealthy individuals.

This awakening is painful because it forces soft-hearted people to confront a difficult truth:

Goodness alone is not sufficient protection.

Some people become emotionally hardened after pain—not because they were born cruel, but because repeated disappointment slowly convinced them that softness was dangerous.

After enough betrayal, rejection, humiliation, or emotional exhaustion, the heart begins building walls for protection. What once felt open and trusting gradually becomes guarded and defensive.

Yet there is a difference between protection and bitterness.

A person can protect their peace without losing kindness. They can develop wisdom without becoming emotionally cold. Healing does not require becoming emotionally empty or suspicious of everyone. True healing allows a person to remain compassionate while also learning discernment, boundaries, and self-respect.

One of the greatest emotional victories in life is not merely surviving pain, but refusing to let pain transform you into someone you never wanted to become.

This chapter explores how emotionally kind individuals learn discernment without losing compassion, and how softness, when guided by wisdom, can become one of the strongest forms of emotional strength.

In This Chapter

This chapter explores the emotional journey of kindhearted individuals who gradually learn that compassion without discernment can lead to repeated emotional injury. It examines emotional overgiving, manipulation, misplaced empathy, boundary failure, emotional exhaustion, fear after emotional injury, bitterness, forgiveness, gratitude, healing, and the development of emotionally wise softness.

The chapter also explains how emotionally healthy discernment allows a person to remain compassionate without becoming emotionally vulnerable to repeated harm.

Chapter Outline

Chapter Overview

Kindness is one of the most valuable human qualities. Compassion, empathy, patience, generosity, and emotional warmth strengthen relationships, communities, and emotional healing. However, kindness becomes psychologically vulnerable when it exists without discernment.

Many emotionally soft individuals struggle to recognize manipulation, emotional exploitation, dishonesty, or destructive relational patterns because they instinctively focus on understanding others rather than evaluating danger. As a result, they often remain in emotionally harmful situations far longer than emotionally discerning individuals would.

This chapter examines how soft-hearted individuals become emotionally overextended, why they frequently attract emotionally wounded or manipulative people, and how repeated emotional injury eventually forces an awakening regarding boundaries, accountability, emotional self-protection, and healing.

Most importantly, this chapter explains that discernment does not destroy kindness.

Discernment protects kindness from destruction.

Many people who experience deep emotional hurt eventually become afraid of vulnerability itself. Emotional defenses slowly develop as survival mechanisms. Some of these defenses are healthy and necessary. Others slowly transform pain into bitterness, suspicion, emotional aggression, or emotional numbness.

This chapter focuses on one of the most important stages of emotional healing: learning how to remain soft-hearted without becoming defenseless.

A healed person learns how to protect peace without becoming cruel, guarded without becoming cold, and emotionally wise without losing compassion.

12.1 The Beautiful Assumption of the Soft Heart

Kindhearted individuals often begin with a beautiful emotional assumption:

> "If I treat people well, they will treat me well too."

This belief reflects emotional sincerity and moral hopefulness. Soft-hearted people tend to project their own intentions onto others. Because they value honesty, empathy, loyalty, and emotional fairness internally, they unconsciously expect similar values externally.

As a result, they often overlook warning signs initially.

They may ignore:

- disrespect,
- manipulation,
- emotional inconsistency,
- dishonesty,
- selfishness,
- or emotional cruelty,

because they instinctively search for the good inside people.

Many compassionate individuals become highly skilled at understanding other people's pain while remaining dangerously unskilled at recognizing emotional danger itself.

Their empathy becomes externally focused while self-protection remains underdeveloped.

This imbalance creates vulnerability.

12.2 When Compassion Becomes Self-Neglect

Soft-hearted individuals frequently confuse self-sacrifice with love.

Because they value compassion deeply, they may tolerate repeated emotional harm while convincing themselves they are simply being patient, understanding, forgiving, or supportive.

Over time, compassion slowly turns into self-neglect.

The individual may continuously excuse harmful behavior by focusing on:

- the other person's trauma,
- difficult childhood,
- emotional wounds,
- insecurity,
- stress,
- or suffering.

While empathy itself is healthy, compassion becomes dangerous when it repeatedly ignores accountability.

Some kindhearted people become so focused on helping others heal that they stop protecting their own emotional well-being entirely.

They absorb:

- emotional chaos,
- disrespect,
- manipulation,
- criticism,
- guilt,
- or emotional instability,

while believing enduring suffering proves emotional maturity or love.

But emotional self-destruction is not compassion.

A healthy heart does not require permanent emotional exhaustion to prove kindness.

Over time, repeated emotional instability can quietly reshape the way a person experiences relationships. Constant exposure to conflict, dependency, manipulation, or emotional unpredictability gradually creates emotional fatigue.

The person who once approached relationships openly may slowly become more cautious, guarded, and selective about who they allow close to them emotionally.

After certain experiences, I noticed this change within myself. I found myself gravitating toward emotionally stable, secure, and self-sufficient individuals because repeated emotional chaos and instability had become deeply exhausting for me.

What once appeared compassionate no longer felt emotionally safe.

I became increasingly afraid of relationships built upon survival pressure, emotional dependency, instability, manipulation, or repeated cycles of emotional exhaustion.

12.3 Why Soft Hearts Attract Emotionally Wounded People

Emotionally soft individuals often attract emotionally wounded people because softness feels emotionally safe.

Compassionate individuals tend to:

- listen patiently,
- forgive repeatedly,
- avoid harsh judgment,
- offer emotional support,
- and create emotional comfort for others.

To emotionally wounded individuals, this can feel deeply relieving.

However, emotionally wounded people who refuse accountability may unconsciously begin depending excessively upon the soft-hearted person's emotional availability. Over time, the relationship becomes emotionally unequal.

The soft-hearted person gives:

- emotional energy,
- understanding,
- patience,
- reassurance,
- forgiveness,
- and emotional labor continuously,

while receiving emotional instability in return.

In some situations, manipulative individuals intentionally seek compassionate people because compassionate people are often easier to guilt, emotionally pressure, or emotionally exploit.

This does not mean kindness is weakness.
It means kindness without discernment becomes vulnerable to misuse.

12.4 The Difficulty of Seeing Evil Clearly

One painful challenge for emotionally kind individuals is recognizing that some people knowingly cause harm.

Soft-hearted people often search for hidden innocence inside destructive behavior. They may repeatedly reinterpret manipulation as misunderstanding, cruelty as woundedness, or exploitation as emotional confusion.

Part of this happens because emotionally healthy individuals struggle psychologically to imagine intentionally harmful motives in others.

They ask:

> "Surely they did not mean it that way."
> "Maybe they were just hurting."
> "Perhaps if I love them enough, they will change."

While these responses reflect compassion, they sometimes prevent realistic judgment.

Not every harmful person is simply misunderstood.

Some individuals repeatedly manipulate, dominate, exploit, deceive, or emotionally injure others while fully aware of the harm they create.

Discernment requires emotionally accepting reality even when reality feels painful.

Kindness must learn to recognize danger honestly instead of endlessly rewriting it into innocence.

12.5 The Awakening — When the Soft Heart Finally Sees

For many kindhearted individuals, awakening comes through repeated pain.

After enough betrayal, emotional exhaustion, manipulation, disappointment, or relational collapse, the person slowly realizes:

"My kindness alone cannot heal everyone."
"Not everyone values empathy."
"Some people use compassion against me."
"I must protect my peace too."

This realization is emotionally painful because it often feels like the loss of innocence itself.

The soft-hearted individual begins grieving:

- misplaced trust,
- ignored warning signs,
- emotional overgiving,
- lost years,
- emotional depletion,
- or relationships built entirely on imbalance.

At first, this awakening may produce bitterness, emotional shutdown, or distrust toward everyone.

But healthy awakening eventually matures into discernment rather than hardness.

The goal is not becoming emotionally cold.
The goal is learning how to remain kind wisely.

12.6 The Hidden Fear After Emotional Injury

One of the deepest fears after emotional injury is the fear of becoming vulnerable again.

Many wounded individuals silently think:

"If I become soft again, I will be hurt again."

This fear is understandable. Emotional pain teaches the brain to anticipate danger. When someone experiences repeated criticism, betrayal, abandonment, emotional instability, or humiliation, the nervous system begins associating emotional openness with risk.

Over time, emotional defenses slowly become automatic. A person may become distant in conversations, suspicious of other people's motives, or overly defensive during even minor disagreements.

At first, these reactions often feel protective.

However, what originally developed as protection can slowly become a prison.

The wounded person may survive the original pain while gradually losing emotional warmth, trust, joy, gentleness, and healthy connection with others.

The tragedy is not only the original wound itself.

The deeper tragedy occurs when the wound reshapes the person's entire emotional character.

In some situations, compassion itself becomes entangled with pressure, guilt, fear, or emotional manipulation. A person may slowly begin feeling responsible for rescuing, carrying, or emotionally stabilizing everyone around them.

Over time, this emotional burden can become psychologically exhausting, especially when kindness is repeatedly met with dependency, pressure, instability, or manipulation rather than mutual responsibility and respect.

I eventually began recognizing this pattern within my own experiences.

At times, I received messages suggesting that if I did not continue helping certain people financially or emotionally, something bad might happen to me spiritually or personally. Experiences like this revealed how compassion can sometimes attract guilt, fear-based pressure, emotional dependency, or manipulation.

For a long time, I carried the emotional weight of believing I was responsible for helping and carrying more than I realistically could. Eventually, however, I realized that compassion without boundaries slowly becomes emotional exhaustion.

Genuine kindness should come from love, wisdom, and free choice — not fear, intimidation, guilt, or emotional coercion.

After certain experiences, I noticed myself becoming more cautious about forming new relationships. I found myself gravitating toward emotionally stable, secure, and self-sufficient individuals because repeated exposure to instability, dependency, and emotional chaos had become deeply exhausting for me.

Looking back, I realized this caution was not truly about status or financial success itself.

It was about emotional safety.

It was about trust.

It was about the fear of being emotionally drained, manipulated, or trapped inside unhealthy relational cycles again.

Over time, I began valuing peace, stability, emotional safety, and emotionally healthy relationships far more deeply than emotional intensity or constant relational instability.

12.7 The Difference Between Softness and Weakness

Many emotionally wounded individuals begin confusing softness with weakness. Because they associate gentleness with vulnerability, they start believing emotional hardness is the only way to stay safe.

But softness is not weakness.
A calm person is not powerless.
A gentle person is not naïve.
A peaceful person is not incapable of strength.

In reality, emotional self-control often requires far greater strength than emotional aggression.

"A person without self-control is like a city with broken-down walls."
— Proverbs 25:28

True emotional maturity is the ability to feel pain without becoming destructive. It is the ability to establish boundaries without hatred, walk away without revenge, and speak truth without cruelty.

The strongest people are not always the loudest or harshest.

Sometimes the strongest individuals are those who maintain compassion even after suffering deeply.

12.8 Boundaries Are Not the Opposite of Love

One of the most important lessons for soft-hearted individuals is understanding that boundaries are not cruelty.

Boundaries protect emotional health.

Many compassionate people fear boundaries because they worry boundaries make them selfish, harsh, unloving, or emotionally unavailable.

However, boundaries are emotional structure.

Without boundaries, emotionally unstable or destructive patterns often continue indefinitely. Some individuals repeatedly manipulate conversations, escalate conflict, drain emotional energy, or create constant psychological chaos around others.

Healthy boundaries allow a person to protect emotional stability without becoming hateful.

Boundaries allow a person to say:

> "I care about you, but I cannot continue unhealthy patterns."
> "I wish you healing, but I will not participate in emotional destruction."
> "My compassion does not require abandoning myself."

Sometimes the healthiest sentence a person can say is:

> "I cannot continue this pattern anymore."

That statement is not cruelty.
It is emotional wisdom.
Boundaries do not destroy compassion.
They preserve it.

One painful realization for many compassionate people is how quickly kindness can become expected rather than appreciated. The moment they establish limits, say no, create boundaries, or become unable to continue helping, they may suddenly be labeled selfish, uncaring, ungrateful, cold, or lacking compassion.

This emotional reversal can feel deeply confusing because the person's value was quietly being measured not by their humanity, but by their continued usefulness, emotional availability, or willingness to sacrifice themselves endlessly.

Over time, many soft-hearted individuals begin realizing that some relationships were built less on mutual care and more on emotional dependency, expectation, or entitlement.

Healthy compassion does not require permanent self-erasure.

A person can be kind while still recognizing their emotional, financial, psychological, and personal limits.

Sometimes the fear of being labeled selfish, uncaring, or ungrateful causes compassionate people to keep giving far beyond healthy limits. They continue trying, helping, rescuing, fixing, explaining, sacrificing, and carrying emotional burdens long after exhaustion has already begun.

Not always because they are strong.
Sometimes because they are afraid of becoming the "bad person" in someone else's story.

Over time, this creates deep emotional fatigue. The person slowly realizes they have been surviving through emotional overextension rather than living with balance, peace, and healthy boundaries.

Compassion should not require the destruction of the self in order to prove its sincerity.

12.9 Discernment — The Wisdom That Protects Kindness

Discernment is the ability to recognize emotional reality clearly.

It involves observing:

- patterns,
- motives,
- consistency,
- accountability,
- manipulation,
- emotional health,
- and relational safety realistically.

Discernment asks:

- Does this person take responsibility?
- Do their actions match their words?
- Do they respect boundaries?
- Do they repeatedly create emotional harm?
- Is this relationship emotionally safe?

Soft-hearted individuals sometimes resist discernment because discernment initially feels judgmental or emotionally uncomfortable.

But discernment is not hatred.
Discernment is emotional wisdom.

A discerning heart still possesses compassion, empathy, patience, and generosity. The difference is that compassion now operates alongside awareness instead of innocence alone.

Wisdom teaches kindness where to remain open and where to step back safely.

12.10 When Protection Turns Into Bitterness

There is an important difference between healthy protection and bitterness.

Healthy protection says:
"I need to protect my peace."

Bitterness says:
"Nobody deserves my kindness anymore."

Healthy boundaries are calm, intentional, and emotionally controlled.

Bitterness, however, is emotionally reactive. It develops when pain remains unresolved for long periods of time.

Repeated disappointment, emotional exhaustion, unresolved anger, and accumulated resentment gradually shape the way a person views people and life itself.

Eventually, bitterness becomes a lens through which every interaction is interpreted.

Over time, bitterness can produce emotional coldness and psychological exhaustion.

The individual who was once wounded may eventually begin wounding others in similar ways.

This is why emotional healing matters so deeply.
Without healing, pain often reproduces itself through behavior.

12.11 Forgiveness Does Not Mean Returning to Harm

Forgiveness is one of the most misunderstood aspects of healing.

Many people assume forgiveness means pretending nothing happened, removing accountability, or immediately restoring trust.

But forgiveness does not mean approving harmful behavior.
It does not mean forgetting abuse or allowing repeated mistreatment.

Forgiveness primarily frees the injured person from remaining emotionally imprisoned by the pain.

Without forgiveness, resentment often becomes psychologically consuming.

The original harm continues living inside the nervous system long after the event itself has ended.

Forgiveness interrupts this cycle.

"Create in me a clean heart, O God, and renew a right spirit within me."
— Psalm 51:10

Forgiveness does not always restore relationships.

Sometimes forgiveness simply means releasing emotional poison so it no longer controls the future.

Over time, I began realizing this personally through certain painful experiences in my own life.

At one point, I experienced public media reporting that I felt misrepresented me unfairly and caused significant emotional pain. For a period of time, I carried deep hurt from the experience. The emotional weight stayed with me far longer than the actual event itself.

Eventually, however, I realized that continuing to carry the pain would only allow the wound to remain alive inside me.

As time passed, I began considering that behind many harmful actions are often people carrying their own fears, pressures, responsibilities, survival struggles, or personal burdens. I considered the possibility that financial pressure, professional pressure, or personal hardship may also have influenced the situation in ways I could not fully see.

Whether or not I completely understood the reasons, I eventually reached a point where I no longer wanted bitterness to control my inner life.

Forgiveness did not mean I believed the harm was acceptable.

It meant I no longer wanted the wound itself to continue shaping my emotional world.

12.12 Gratitude as a Psychological Reorientation

One of the most powerful healing processes is gratitude.

Emotionally wounded individuals often become psychologically trapped in what was missing, unfair, painful, or disappointing.

Gratitude slowly redirects emotional attention toward stability instead of absence.

Healing often begins with small recognitions:

- food to eat,
- shoes on one's feet,
- a safe place to sleep,
- supportive people,
- moments of peace,
- and opportunities to rebuild.

Gratitude changes emotional orientation.

Instead of asking:

"What did life fail to give me?"

the person slowly begins asking:

"What remains good, stable, meaningful, or valuable in my life?"

This shift weakens bitterness by restoring perspective.

12.13 Refusing to Become the Pain

One of the most important moments in healing occurs when a person consciously decides:

"I do not want this pain to define who I become."

Some wounded individuals eventually recognize they are beginning to resemble the very behaviors that once hurt them.

Healing often starts when a person becomes emotionally honest enough to say:

"I do not want to continue this cycle."
"I want peace."
"I do not want my pain spreading into other people's lives."
"I want emotional stability."

The refusal to become emotionally destructive despite suffering is one of the clearest signs of growing emotional maturity.

12.14 Emotional Healing Requires Repetition

Healing is rarely immediate.

Emotional patterns formed through years of pain, instability, fear, or survival usually require repeated correction over time.

Some days a person feels emotionally strong and peaceful.
Other days old reactions return unexpectedly.
This does not necessarily mean healing has failed.
It often means the emotional system is still learning new patterns.
Healing usually involves repeated practices such as:

- self-reflection,
- emotional regulation,
- prayer,
- gratitude,
- counseling,
- healthy communication,
- journaling,
- and avoiding emotionally destructive environments.

Healing is often less about perfection and more about consistent movement toward emotional health.

12.15 Remaining Soft Without Remaining Naïve

Some wounded individuals respond to betrayal by becoming emotionally hardened completely.

They stop trusting.
Stop opening emotionally.
Stop believing in goodness.

But this response creates a different form of suffering.

The goal of healing is not emotional numbness.
The goal is emotionally wise softness.

A hardened person says:

> "Nobody can hurt me anymore."

A healed person says:

> "I know how to protect my peace now."

A healed person still possesses compassion, empathy, and emotional warmth, but also develops discernment.

They learn when to trust, when to step back, and when to protect emotional stability.

True emotional maturity combines both compassion and discernment simultaneously.

A soft heart protected by wisdom becomes emotionally resilient rather than emotionally fragile.

Healing is not the loss of softness.
Healing is softness strengthened by wisdom.

12.16 The Victory of the Soft Heart

One of the greatest emotional tests for a soft-hearted person is learning how to remain emotionally stable after being deeply hurt by emotionally destructive individuals.

Some people eventually attack the very person who tried to help them.

They may spread accusations, damage reputations, distort events, manipulate others, or attempt to emotionally destroy those who once showed them kindness.

For many soft-hearted individuals, this experience is deeply shocking because they never imagined that compassion could be repaid with hostility.

The pain becomes even greater when the damage affects reputation, relationships, emotional peace, or public perception.

At this stage, bitterness becomes a temptation.

The wounded person may feel the urge to retaliate, obsess over revenge, expose every flaw, or emotionally harden themselves against the world.

But becoming consumed by bitterness only continues the cycle of emotional destruction.

The emotionally mature soft-hearted person eventually realizes:

> "I cannot control what bitterness produced in them, but I can refuse to let it reproduce itself inside me."

This realization does not deny the damage.

It does not require weakness, silence, or the absence of boundaries.

Instead, it reflects a refusal to allow pain to transform one's character into the very thing that caused the suffering.

Even after betrayal, false accusations, humiliation, or damaged reputation, emotional strength is ultimately revealed through stability, restraint, wisdom, and self-control.

A soft heart protected by wisdom does not become naïve.
But neither does it become poisoned by hatred.
The final victory of the soft-hearted person is not revenge.
It is remaining emotionally whole without becoming what wounded them.

12.17 Protecting the Heart Without Becoming Bitter

A soft heart should not become a self-destructive heart.

Many kind people eventually face a painful question:

> "How do I remain loving without allowing myself to be repeatedly wounded?"

Some respond by becoming emotionally closed, distrustful, harsh, or bitter. Others continue giving endlessly without boundaries until emotional exhaustion consumes them.

Neither path creates lasting peace.
True emotional maturity is not found in becoming cold.

It is found in learning how to remain compassionate while also becoming discerning.

Forgiveness does not mean pretending the harm never happened.

It does not require restoring broken trust, reopening harmful access, or remaining trapped in destructive cycles.

Some individuals may never fully heal from their bitterness, resentment, instability, or destructive behaviors. Some repeatedly damage the very people who loved, supported, protected, or sacrificed for them.

The soft-hearted person must eventually understand:

> loving others does not require abandoning wisdom.

Boundaries are not hatred.

Distance is not revenge.
Discernment is not cruelty.
Self-protection is not selfishness.

A healed soft-hearted person learns to forgive without surrendering peace. They learn to release bitterness without returning to destruction.

They learn to remain gentle without remaining vulnerable to every harmful person they encounter.

The goal is not to lose compassion.
The goal is to protect compassion from becoming consumed by emotionally destructive patterns.

A soft heart guided by wisdom becomes far stronger than a hard heart driven by pain.

Key Insight

Healing is not becoming emotionally empty.

Healing is learning how to remain kind without becoming vulnerable to repeated emotional destruction.

A healed person does not lose compassion. They simply learn where compassion must be balanced with wisdom, boundaries, discernment, and self-respect.

Kindness without discernment becomes vulnerable to manipulation, exhaustion, and emotional collapse.

Discernment does not destroy compassion.

It protects compassion from being consumed by emotionally unhealthy people.

Summary

This chapter explored how emotionally kind individuals often become vulnerable to emotional manipulation, overgiving, self-neglect, and repeated emotional injury when compassion exists without discernment. It examined emotional innocence, misplaced empathy, emotional exploitation, boundaries, awakening through pain, fear after emotional injury, forgiveness, gratitude, bitterness, healing, and the development of emotionally wise softness.

The chapter also emphasized that discernment is not cruelty or emotional hardness. Rather, discernment allows compassionate individuals to remain emotionally open while also protecting themselves from repeated harm.

Ultimately, healing involves learning how to preserve kindness without abandoning emotional wisdom, boundaries, or self-respect.

Conclusion

Pain changes people.
The deeper question is whether pain will make a person wiser or merely harder.

A person can suffer deeply without becoming cruel.
A person can develop boundaries without becoming emotionally cold.
A person can protect peace without losing kindness.

Healing is not the loss of softness.
Healing is softness strengthened by wisdom.
A soft heart is not weak.

But softness without discernment becomes vulnerable in a world where not every person values empathy, honesty, or emotional responsibility equally.

Many compassionate individuals spend years trying to heal people who continuously wound them because they confuse self-sacrifice with love.

Eventually, life teaches them a painful but necessary truth:
Kindness must learn discernment if it wishes to survive.
The healthiest heart is neither cold nor naïve.
It is compassionate, wise, emotionally awake, and emotionally protected.

Ending Reflection

The awakening of the soft heart is painful because it often begins with disappointment.

The person slowly realizes that good intentions alone cannot protect against manipulation, exploitation, or emotional harm.

At first, this realization may feel like the loss of innocence itself.

But true awakening is not the death of kindness.
It is the maturation of kindness.

The awakened heart still loves deeply, cares sincerely, and values compassion. The difference is that wisdom now stands beside compassion, protecting it from destruction.

A soft heart does not need to become hard to survive.

It simply needs discernment.
A healed heart is not a defenseless heart.

It is a heart that has learned how to remain kind while no longer surrendering itself to emotional destruction.

Ending Quotes

"Be wise as serpents and innocent as doves."
— Matthew 10:16

"Above all else, guard your heart, for everything you do flows from it."
— Proverbs 4:23

"Better a patient person than a warrior, one with self-control than one who takes a city."
— Proverbs 16:32

"Do not be overcome by evil, but overcome evil with good."
— Romans 12:21

"Compassion without discernment eventually becomes exhaustion."
— Levi Sap Nei Thang

"Healing is not becoming hard enough that nothing touches you. Healing is learning what deserves access to your heart."
— Levi Sap Nei Thang

"The goal is not to stop being kind. The goal is to stop abandoning yourself in the name of kindness."
— Levi Sap Nei Thang

Reflection Questions

1. Have you ever believed that kindness alone would protect you from emotional harm?
2. Do you tend to focus more on understanding other people's pain than protecting your own emotional well-being?
3. Have you ever remained in a relationship, friendship, or situation long after it became emotionally unhealthy?
4. Are there warning signs you ignored because you hoped someone would eventually change?
5. Have you ever confused self-sacrifice with love or emotional maturity?
6. What situations in your life have taught you the importance of boundaries?
7. Do you struggle with guilt when saying no, creating distance, or protecting your peace?
8. Have you ever feared becoming emotionally soft again after being hurt deeply?
9. In what ways has emotional pain changed how you trust, connect with, or open yourself to others?
10. What does a healthy boundary look like for you personally?
11. Are there relationships in your life where compassion exists without enough accountability or mutual care?
12. Have you ever worried that protecting yourself would make you selfish, cold, or unkind?
13. What emotional habits or patterns are you no longer willing to tolerate in your life?
14. What does emotionally wise softness mean to you personally?
15. How can you remain compassionate without abandoning yourself emotionally?
16. What would healing look like if kindness and wisdom worked together in your life instead of opposing each other?

Conclusion

Patterns rarely appear all at once. They emerge gradually through repetition—through reactions that seem temporary, conflicts that seem isolated, emotional responses that appear understandable, and behaviors that initially feel necessary for survival or protection. Over time, repeated cycles begin revealing structure. What once appeared situational becomes predictable. What once felt accidental begins repeating with increasing consistency across relationships, environments, and stages of life. Repeated conflict is rarely random. A pattern becomes visible when different situations repeatedly produce the same outcome.

This book was written to make those patterns visible.
Not to encourage condemnation.
Not to simplify human complexity.
And not to reduce people to labels.

Human beings are shaped by experiences, environments, attachment, deprivation, instability, rejection, emotional conditioning, survival, opportunity, and relationships. Many behaviors discussed throughout this book originate not from inherent cruelty alone, but from adaptation. What once protected a person emotionally in unstable conditions may later continue operating long after the original environment has changed. What begins as survival can become identity when it is never allowed to heal.

But understanding origin does not remove impact.

Unresolved hardship often continues speaking through behavior long after words have stopped. Unresolved patterns affect relationships, trust, communication, emotional safety, identity, families, workplaces, communities, and systems of support. Pain that remains unhealed often spreads outward relationally. Without awareness, emotional survival systems continue repeating—not always because individuals consciously desire destruction, but because repetition gradually becomes psychologically structured and emotionally familiar. Some people escape poverty externally while remaining trapped in survival internally.

Recognition changes participation.

Once patterns become visible, it becomes possible to respond with greater clarity rather than confusion. People become less vulnerable to cycles of manipulation, emotional exhaustion, instability, escalation, bitterness, relational collapse, and repeated psychological harm. They gain the ability to establish boundaries without unnecessary hatred, maintain emotional stability without losing compassion, and disengage from destructive cycles without surrendering their humanity.

At the same time, recognition also creates the possibility of healing.

Patterns that were learned can also be interrupted. Survival teaches protection. Healing teaches regulation. Survival-based responses that once operated automatically can gradually be replaced with awareness, accountability, emotional regulation, discernment, repair, forgiveness, gratitude, boundaries, humility, emotional wisdom, and healthier forms of connection. Change is rarely immediate, but repetition works in both directions. Just as instability becomes reinforced through repetition, emotional healing and stability can also strengthen through repeated intentional choices over time. Healing does not erase the past. It changes the future.

The goal of this book is therefore not merely observation. It is clarity.

Because clarity allows people to distinguish:

- intensity from strength,
- control from stability,
- manipulation from influence,
- emotional hardness from emotional maturity,
- compassion from self-neglect,
- survival from healing,
- and reaction from intentional response.

Intensity attracts attention. Stability sustains relationships. Not all confidence reflects emotional clarity. The strongest structures are not built on fear, but on stability. A soft heart protected by wisdom is stronger than a hardened heart ruled by fear. Discernment protects compassion from becoming self-destruction. The goal is not emotional numbness. The goal is emotional wisdom.

Not every cycle can be repaired through continued participation. Not every relationship becomes healthy through patience alone. And not every pattern should be normalized simply because it has become familiar.

Sometimes the most important transformation begins when a person finally recognizes:

> The environment changed, but the internal system never did.

That realization can become the beginning of emotional awakening. From that moment forward, a different direction becomes possible. Healing becomes possible.

And perhaps most importantly, a healed person is not someone who never suffered. A healed person is someone who learned how to suffer without becoming cruel.

Final Quote

A healed person is not someone who never suffered.

A healed person is someone who learned how to suffer without becoming cruel.
— Levi Sap Nei Thang

"Wisdom does not destroy kindness. Wisdom teaches kindness where to stand."
— Levi Sap Nei Thang

"Boundaries are not cruelty. They are emotional responsibility."
— Levi Sap Nei Thang

"Compassion without wisdom may invite repeated harm. Wisdom without compassion may harden the heart."
— Levi Sap Nei Thang

"Peace is difficult to maintain when emotional wounds continue controlling present relationships."
— Levi Sap Nei Thang

"Not every form of strength is healthy. Some forms of strength are simply pain that learned how to survive loudly."
— Levi Sap Nei Thang

"When bitterness remains unresolved, survival can slowly replace empathy."
— Levi Sap Nei Thang

"A person may appear powerful externally while still being emotionally ruled by unresolved wounds internally."
— Levi Sap Nei Thang

"Emotional hardness is not always strength. Sometimes it is unhealed pain wearing armor."
— Levi Sap Nei Thang

"Without discernment, intimidation may be mistaken for confidence, and cruelty may be mistaken for power."
— Levi Sap Nei Thang

"Some people admire survival-driven success because they see in it an escape from their own feelings of weakness, poverty, or insignificance."
— Levi Sap Nei Thang

"The desire to never feel powerless again can slowly transform self-protection into selfishness."
— Levi Sap Nei Thang

"Not every admired person is emotionally healthy. Public admiration and emotional maturity are not the same thing."
— Levi Sap Nei Thang

"When validation becomes a substitute for healing, success alone can never create peace."
— Levi Sap Nei Thang

"People who are emotionally starving may mistake dominance for security and aggression for leadership."
— Levi Sap Nei Thang

"Unresolved shame often hides behind excessive pride, control, defensiveness, or the constant need to appear superior."
— Levi Sap Nei Thang

"Some individuals do not heal from suffering. They reorganize their personality around surviving it."
— Levi Sap Nei Thang

"The wounded person may seek power not to lead others, but to avoid ever feeling weak again."
— Levi Sap Nei Thang

"Financial success can improve circumstances, but it cannot automatically heal bitterness, resentment, or emotional instability."
— Levi Sap Nei Thang

"The most dangerous dysfunctions are often the ones society rewards with applause, influence, money, or attention."
— Levi Sap Nei Thang

"A survival-based identity may achieve status externally while remaining emotionally imprisoned internally."
— Levi Sap Nei Thang

"A person who only learned survival may struggle to understand love, peace, stability, or mutual emotional responsibility."
— Levi Sap Nei Thang

"False strength seeks control. Real strength maintains integrity even without control."
— Levi Sap Nei Thang

"The goal of healing is not becoming emotionally cold enough to survive everyone. The goal is learning how to remain compassionate without remaining emotionally unprotected."
— Levi Sap Nei Thang

"Emotional hardness is not always strength. Sometimes it is unhealed pain wearing armor."
— Levi Sap Nei Tha

Behavioral Comparison Table

Area	Pattern-Based Behavior	Stable / Healthy Behavior
Conflict	Escalates quickly; continues beyond issue	Addresses issue, then resolves
Interpretation	Neutral actions seen as threat or opposition	Neutral actions interpreted proportionally
Accountability	Avoided, redirected, or justified	Acknowledged clearly and directly
Repair	Minimal or absent; patterns repeat	Apology, correction, and change follow conflict
Boundaries	Seen as control or hostility	Understood as structure and limits
Communication	Used to pressure, escalate, or dominate	Used to clarify, understand, and resolve
Support	Eventually turned into opposition	Maintained with respect and reciprocity
Reaction to Calm	Discomfort; creates tension	Accepts and maintains stability
Focus	"Who is against me?"	"What is the issue?"
Conflict Spread	Expands across people and situations	Remains contained to specific issue
Attention	Reinforced by visibility and reaction	Not dependent on attention to function
Power / Influence	Used to control direction or narrative	Used to support structure and alignment
Outcome Over Time	Instability, division, erosion	Stability, trust, continuity

Glossary

Accountability
The willingness to acknowledge actions, recognize impact, and accept responsibility without deflection or justification.

Adaptive Aggression
Aggressive behavior developed as a protective response to environments perceived as threatening, unstable, or emotionally unsafe.

Adaptive Behavior
Behavior developed in response to environmental pressure, hardship, or instability that originally served a protective purpose but may later create difficulty when conditions change.

Admiration of Survival-Based Success
The tendency to idealize individuals who appear financially powerful, emotionally dominant, socially influential, or aggressively successful, even when their behavior may be emotionally unhealthy or destructive.

Aggressive Defensiveness
A defensive reaction in which individuals respond to perceived criticism, disagreement, or vulnerability through confrontation, hostility, or intensified opposition.

Alienation
A state of emotional or social disconnection in which individuals feel separated from others, unsupported, misunderstood, or excluded from meaningful belonging.

Alignment
A state in which actions, communication, values, and responsibilities function consistently together, allowing relationships, teams, or systems to operate with stability and trust.

Ambiguous Threat Interpretation
The tendency to interpret unclear, neutral, or uncertain situations as potentially hostile, critical, or dangerous.

Ambition
The drive to pursue achievement, influence, recognition, or advancement.

Attachment
An emotional bond formed between individuals that influences trust, intimacy, emotional security, dependence, vulnerability, and relational behavior.

Attention Reinforcement
The strengthening of repeated behavior through visibility, reaction, emotional engagement, or ongoing public focus.

Authority Conflict
Recurring tension with figures, systems, or structures associated with leadership, boundaries, accountability, or control.

Awareness
The ability to observe one's own thoughts, behaviors, emotional reactions, and patterns with clarity rather than automatic response.

Behavioral Pattern
A repeated and recognizable way of responding, reacting, or interacting across multiple situations over time.

Bitterness
A prolonged emotional state characterized by unresolved resentment, disappointment, or anger resulting from perceived unfairness, hardship, betrayal, or repeated emotional injury.

Boundaries
Clearly defined emotional, relational, or behavioral limits that protect stability, respect, and personal well-being.

Boundary-Based Healing
A healing process that combines compassion with emotional limits, accountability, discernment, and self-respect in order to prevent repeated emotional harm.

Boundary Resistance
The tendency to interpret limits, accountability, or structure as rejection, hostility, or control rather than as healthy relational guidance.

Chronic Conflict
A repeated pattern of unresolved tension or disagreement that persists across multiple interactions, relationships, or environments over time.

Communication Breakdown
The gradual loss of effective dialogue due to repeated escalation, defensiveness, distrust, or emotional tension.

Comparison
The process of evaluating oneself against others, often based on status, success, opportunity, recognition, or material conditions.

Compassion Fatigue
A state of emotional exhaustion caused by prolonged caregiving, emotional overgiving, repeated exposure to suffering, or continuous emotional support without sufficient recovery or reciprocity.

Compassion Without Discernment
A pattern in which empathy and kindness are extended without recognizing harmful behaviors, emotional manipulation, instability, or repeated relational damage.

Conflict Dependency
A psychological reliance on conflict, tension, or opposition as a source of emotional stimulation, identity, structure, or direction.

Conflict Structure
A psychological pattern in which conflict becomes emotionally organizing, providing familiarity, identity, or direction rather than functioning as a temporary disagreement.

Conscience
The internal moral awareness that produces sensitivity toward empathy, guilt, accountability, right and wrong, emotional harm, and relational responsibility.

Control
The attempt to direct, manage, influence, or dominate situations, people, or outcomes in ways that reduce uncertainty or emotional discomfort.

Defensiveness
An emotional or behavioral response aimed at protecting oneself from criticism, vulnerability, accountability, or perceived threat.

Deflection
The redirection of attention away from the original issue or responsibility toward secondary reactions or unrelated concerns.

Defensive Self-Importance
An exaggerated need to appear strong, superior, respected, untouchable, or important in order to psychologically defend against feelings of shame, weakness, insecurity, rejection, or humiliation.

Dependency
An unhealthy emotional reliance upon another person for validation, emotional regulation, identity, security, stability, or self-worth.

Destabilization
The gradual weakening of emotional, relational, or organizational stability through repeated tension, escalation, inconsistency, or unresolved conflict.

Dignity Loss
A psychological experience in which repeated hardship, humiliation, exclusion, or dependency weakens a person's sense of self-worth, value, or personal significance.

Discernment
The ability to recognize emotional reality clearly, including patterns, motives, manipulation, accountability, relational safety, emotional health, and psychological danger.

Disengagement
The intentional reduction of participation in repeated patterns of escalation, instability, or harmful interaction.

Disruption
An interruption of stability, communication, trust, or functional structure within relationships, environments, or systems.

Emotional Accountability
The practice of taking responsibility for emotional behavior, communication patterns, reactions, and relational impact without constant deflection or blame.

Emotional Aggression
Behavior intended to intimidate, humiliate, dominate, manipulate, destabilize, or psychologically harm another person emotionally.

Emotional Boundaries
Psychological, emotional, and relational limits that protect an individual's mental well-being, self-respect, peace, and emotional safety within relationships.

Emotional Burnout
A state of emotional depletion caused by prolonged psychological stress, chronic instability, caregiving overload, unresolved conflict, or repeated emotional strain.

Emotional Conditioning
The shaping of emotional responses through repeated experiences, environments, or interactions over time.

Emotional Deprivation
The prolonged absence of emotional support, reassurance, affection, or psychological safety during important developmental periods.

Emotional Desensitization
The gradual weakening of empathy, emotional responsiveness, guilt, moral discomfort, or conscience after repeated exposure to aggression, cruelty, instability, or emotional harm.

Emotional Discernment
The ability to accurately recognize the difference between genuine strength and emotionally unhealthy behavior, including manipulation, intimidation, cruelty, or survival-based aggression.

Emotional Displacement
The unconscious redirection of unresolved anger, shame, resentment, frustration, or emotional pain onto safer or unrelated individuals.

Emotional Exhaustion
A state of mental and emotional depletion caused by prolonged stress, instability, unresolved conflict, or chronic tension.

Emotional Exploitation
The manipulation or use of another person's empathy, kindness, support, forgiveness, loyalty, or emotional openness for personal gain, control, attention, or advantage.

Emotional Guardedness
A protective emotional posture characterized by caution, distrust, distance, or reluctance to become emotionally vulnerable.

Emotional Hardening
A gradual reduction in emotional sensitivity, empathy, vulnerability, or compassion caused by repeated pain, disappointment, humiliation, betrayal, or survival stress.

Emotional Hypervigilance
A persistent state of psychological alertness in which the nervous system constantly scans for danger, betrayal, instability, criticism, rejection, or emotional harm.

Emotional Instability
Difficulty maintaining consistent emotional regulation, often resulting in rapid shifts in mood, reaction, or interpersonal behavior.

Emotional Manipulation
The use of guilt, fear, shame, emotional pressure, deception, withdrawal, or psychological tactics to influence, control, destabilize, or emotionally dominate another person.

Emotional Numbness
A reduced ability to experience joy, emotional warmth, connection, vulnerability, excitement, or emotional responsiveness due to prolonged stress or survival conditioning.

Emotional Predation
The intentional or unconscious targeting of emotionally vulnerable individuals for domination, exploitation, emotional discharge, manipulation, or psychological control.

Emotional Projection
A defense mechanism in which individuals unconsciously assign their own fears, shame, insecurities, anger, or unresolved emotions onto others.

Emotional Recovery
The gradual restoration of emotional stability, peace, trust, clarity, and psychological well-being after periods of emotional pain, instability, manipulation, betrayal, or relational exhaustion.

Emotional Regulation
The ability to recognize and manage emotional responses without becoming fully controlled by them.

Emotional Sadism
Psychological gratification or emotional satisfaction derived from humiliating, controlling, destabilizing, or emotionally hurting another person.

Emotional Scarcity
A psychological condition in which individuals feel deprived of emotional safety, love, peace, trust, stability, or fulfillment regardless of external circumstances.

Emotional Self-Neglect
The repeated abandonment of one's own emotional needs, well-being, safety, or mental health to prioritize others excessively.

Emotional Self-Protection
The healthy practice of protecting one's emotional well-being through boundaries, wisdom, discernment, accountability, and emotionally responsible decision-making.

Emotional Survival Mode
A prolonged psychological state focused primarily on protection, endurance, vigilance, urgency, and threat management rather than peace, connection, or emotional fulfillment.

Emotional Survival Response
A protective psychological reaction developed in response to prolonged emotional hardship, instability, or perceived threat, which may later persist beyond the original environment.

Emotional Discernment
The ability to recognize the difference between compassion and emotional vulnerability, allowing individuals to remain kind without ignoring harmful patterns or destructive behavior.

Empathy
The ability to emotionally recognize, understand, and respond sensitively to another person's emotions, experiences, or suffering.

Entitlement
The belief that certain treatment, opportunity, recognition, or support is inherently deserved, regardless of reciprocity, accountability, or circumstance.

Escalation
The process through which conflict or emotional intensity increases beyond the original issue.

Escalation Cycle
A repeating sequence in which conflict intensifies through reaction, counterreaction, emotional reinforcement, and lack of resolution.

External Validation
The reliance on attention, approval, recognition, or reaction from others to maintain self-worth, identity, or emotional stability.

False Strength
The appearance of confidence, fearlessness, dominance, aggression, emotional coldness, or intimidation that is mistaken for genuine emotional maturity, wisdom, stability, or character strength.

Financial Survival Conditioning
Psychological patterns formed through prolonged financial insecurity, deprivation, instability, or fear of poverty that continue influencing emotional behavior, relationships, trust, and decision-making even after circumstances improve.

Forgiveness
The process of releasing chronic resentment, bitterness, emotional captivity, or revenge without necessarily removing accountability or restoring unsafe relationships.

Fragmentation
The division of relationships, teams, or communities into opposing sides or disconnected groups due to repeated conflict or instability.

Gratitude
An intentional emotional orientation toward recognizing value, stability, blessings, meaning, or positive aspects of life rather than focusing exclusively on deprivation or loss.

Healing
The gradual process of recognizing, understanding, and changing patterns that no longer support emotional stability or healthy relationships.

Healing-Oriented Forgiveness
Forgiveness practiced for emotional recovery, peace, and psychological healing rather than for enabling continued harmful behavior or avoiding difficult truths.

Healthy Forgiveness
A form of forgiveness that releases bitterness and emotional resentment without denying truth, removing accountability, or abandoning emotional boundaries and self-protection.

Healthy Shame
A morally protective form of emotional discomfort that occurs after harmful behavior and encourages accountability, empathy, and behavioral correction.

Hostility
A pattern of antagonistic, aggressive, or oppositional emotional response toward individuals, groups, or situations.

Hypervigilance
An ongoing state of excessive alertness in which individuals constantly anticipate danger, rejection, betrayal, instability, conflict, or emotional harm.

Identity Formation
The process through which repeated experiences, environments, beliefs, and emotional patterns shape a person's sense of self.

Identity Through Struggle
A condition in which a person becomes psychologically attached to bitterness, victimhood, suffering, conflict, or survival identity because it has become deeply integrated into their sense of self.

Idealization
The psychological tendency to view another person unrealistically positively, often assigning exaggerated emotional significance or expectations to them.

Influence
The ability to shape perception, behavior, decisions, or interaction within relationships, groups, or systems.

Instability
A condition characterized by unpredictability, inconsistency, emotional volatility, or lack of structural security.

Internalized Instability
A condition in which prolonged exposure to unstable environments causes instability to become psychologically normalized and unconsciously expected in future relationships or situations.

Internalization
The process through which repeated external experiences become psychologically embedded, influencing long-term thought patterns, emotional responses, and behavior.

Isolation
A state of emotional, psychological, or social separation from supportive relationships, communities, or systems.

Manipulation
The strategic use of emotional pressure, deception, fear, guilt, shame, emotional withdrawal, or psychological tactics to gain control, advantage, or emotional power over others.

Moral Desensitization
The gradual weakening of empathy, guilt, conscience, or moral discomfort regarding harmful behavior through repetition or repeated exposure.

Narrative Control
The shaping or reframing of situations in ways that influence how others interpret conflict, responsibility, or behavior.

Normalization of Dysfunction
The process by which repeated exposure to unhealthy behavior causes manipulation, cruelty, instability, dishonesty, emotional aggression, or toxic relational patterns to become viewed as normal or acceptable.

Opposition
The interpretation of disagreement or difference as personal resistance or hostility.

Perception
The process through which individuals interpret experiences, relationships, and environments based on both present circumstances and past conditioning.

Poverty Bitterness Syndrome
A behavioral and psychological pattern in which unresolved hardship, deprivation, resentment, survival conditioning, or chronic emotional instability continue shaping perception, relationships, and behavior even after external circumstances change.

Poverty Mindset
A persistent psychological orientation shaped by chronic perceptions of scarcity, insecurity, instability, fear of loss, or survival-based thinking, which may continue even after material conditions improve.

Projection
A psychological process in which unwanted emotions, motivations, or behaviors are attributed to others rather than recognized within oneself.

Reactivity
The tendency to respond impulsively or emotionally to situations without reflection or regulation.

Relational Cycling
A repeated emotional pattern involving attachment, conflict, rupture, reconciliation, instability, and repeated relational tension.

Relational Instability
Persistent emotional inconsistency, unpredictability, volatility, conflict, or dysfunction within interpersonal relationships.

Relational Utility Thinking
A pattern in which relationships are viewed primarily through usefulness, benefit, financial opportunity, emotional supply, status advancement, or personal advantage rather than mutual care and respect.

Remorse
A genuine emotional recognition of wrongdoing accompanied by empathy, regret, guilt, sorrow, or desire for change.

Repair
The restoration of trust or stability after conflict through acknowledgment, accountability, and consistent behavioral change.

Resentment
The prolonged emotional carryover of unresolved anger, perceived unfairness, or repeated hardship.

Scarcity Mentality
A fear-based psychological orientation organized around the belief that safety, stability, love, opportunities, or resources are insufficient or constantly threatened.

Self-Sabotage
Behavior patterns that unconsciously damage emotional stability, relationships, self-worth, goals, or long-term well-being.

Shame
A painful emotional experience involving feelings of defectiveness, humiliation, inadequacy, unworthiness, or moral failure.

Soft-Heartedness
An emotionally compassionate, empathetic, emotionally open, gentle, and relationally caring way of relating to others.

Stability
A condition of emotional, relational, or structural consistency that allows trust, clarity, and continuity to develop over time.

Status-Based Validation
The tendency to measure personal worth primarily through financial success, social influence, public attention, power, dominance, or external recognition.

Strategic Cruelty
The intentional use of humiliation, intimidation, emotional harm, manipulation, or psychological attack to gain power, control, dominance, or emotional advantage.

Survival Conditioning
Behavioral and emotional patterns formed through repeated exposure to hardship, instability, conflict, or insecurity.

Survival Mode
A prolonged emotional and psychological state in which protection, urgency, and adaptation take priority over reflection and stability.

Survival Thinking
A psychological state in which fear, insecurity, deprivation, or instability cause individuals to prioritize self-protection, control, status, or immediate gain above emotional health, ethics, empathy, or long-term relational stability.

Tension Seeking
A tendency to recreate conflict, urgency, or emotional intensity because calm or stability feels unfamiliar or uncomfortable.

Toxic Relationship Pattern
A repeated relational dynamic characterized by manipulation, disrespect, emotional instability, imbalance, exhaustion, hostility, or psychological harm.

Transactional Relationships
Relationships organized primarily around usefulness, obligation, emotional exchange, survival needs, or conditional value rather than mutual emotional intimacy.

Trauma Carryover
The process by which unresolved emotional pain, fear, distrust, or survival behaviors from past experiences continue influencing future relationships and emotional reactions.

Trauma Reenactment
The unconscious repetition of unresolved emotional wounds, relational dynamics, or survival behaviors in future relationships or environments

Trust Erosion
The gradual weakening of confidence, reliability, or emotional safety within relationships or systems due to repeated unresolved conflict or inconsistency.

Validation Dependency
A pattern in which self-worth becomes heavily dependent upon admiration, praise, attention, status, control, social approval, or external recognition from others.

Validation Seeking
The repeated pursuit of recognition, agreement, attention, or affirmation from others to maintain emotional stability or self-worth.

Verbal Escalation
The use of language in ways that increase emotional intensity, pressure, conflict, or instability within interaction.

Vulnerability
The emotional openness involved in honesty, intimacy, trust, emotional exposure, authenticity, or psychological transparency.

Wise Softness
A form of emotional maturity in which compassion, kindness, empathy, and emotional openness remain present while also being protected by discernment, boundaries, and emotional wisdom.

Book Description

Some wounds do not end when hardship ends.

They continue quietly through bitterness, defensiveness, emotional exhaustion, manipulation, fear, unstable relationships, and survival patterns that no longer protect—but instead begin damaging trust, peace, and emotional stability.

This book explores how unresolved survival conditioning can shape human behavior, emotional reactions, identity, and relationships long after the original pain has passed. Through psychological insight, emotional reflection, behavioral analysis, relational dynamics, and spiritual perspective, it examines emotional defensiveness, shame, resentment, overgiving, attachment, relational instability, fear of abandonment, hypervigilance, self-sabotage, and the hidden emotional cycles that silently influence human behavior.

Thought-provoking and deeply reflective, this work explores the tension between survival and healing—and the difficult journey of protecting a soft heart without losing it.

Many people who endure hardship develop resilience, empathy, wisdom, gratitude, integrity, and compassion. This book does not condemn poverty or those who suffer through it. Instead, it examines what can happen when survival mechanisms formed during prolonged suffering remain emotionally active long after the original environment has changed.

It explores how unresolved emotional pain may continue operating beneath visible behavior, influencing relationships, identity, trust, emotional regulation, and perceptions of self and others. The book also examines the difference between external success and internal healing, showing how some individuals may escape poverty financially while remaining emotionally trapped in survival-based thinking.

At the same time, the book strongly emphasizes personal responsibility, accountability, forgiveness, emotional growth, healing, humility, gratitude, and self-awareness. Trauma may explain behavior, but explanation is not the same as justification.

The later chapters focus heavily on recovery, emotional regulation, rebuilding conscience, relational repair, breaking destructive generational patterns, and learning healthier ways to relate to others. Readers are encouraged to approach the subject with both discernment toward destructive behavior and compassion toward human suffering.

This book is about awareness, accountability, healing, discernment, forgiveness, gratitude, emotional wisdom, and learning how to remain compassionate without becoming emotionally unprotected.

It is about what happens when pain hardens rather than heals—and how emotional wounds can silently shape identity, behavior, relationships, and perception long after visible hardship has ended.

But it is also about hope.
Because healing is possible.
Self-awareness is possible.
Forgiveness is possible.
And survival does not have to become destiny.

About the Author

Levi Sap Nei Thang is an author and independent publisher whose work explores behavioral patterns, human psychology, and lived experience.

She holds a Bachelor of Science (BSc) in Physics and a Master of Divinity (MDiv) in Theology, combining analytical discipline with a deep understanding of human values, belief systems, and moral frameworks.

In recognition of her humanitarian contributions, she has also been awarded an Honorary Doctorate in Humanity.

Alongside her academic background, she has been involved in disaster recovery efforts and philanthropic initiatives, working across diverse communities and engaging with people from a wide range of social and economic environments. These experiences have provided her with direct insight into how hardship, instability, and opportunity shape long-term behavioral patterns.

Having served in leadership and high-responsibility roles, she brings both structured analysis and real-world experience to her work—focusing on patterns that are often observed but rarely clearly defined.

Her writing aims to help readers recognize these patterns, understand their impact, and step out of cycles that do not lead to stability.

Disclaimer

This book is intended for educational and reflective purposes only. It does not provide medical, psychological, psychiatric, legal, or clinical diagnosis, treatment, or professional advice. The concepts discussed are presented as behavioral and social observations intended to encourage reflection, awareness, emotional understanding, and personal growth.

The author makes no representations or warranties regarding the accuracy, completeness, or applicability of the contents and shall not be liable for any direct, indirect, incidental, or consequential damages arising from the use of this book.

This work discusses generalized psychological, emotional, and relational patterns for educational and reflective purposes only. Any resemblance to specific individuals, organizations, or events is unintentional. The content is not intended to diagnose, label, defame, or target any particular person or group.

Readers are encouraged to seek qualified professional assistance for medical, psychological, legal, or mental health concerns.

www.ingramcontent.com/pod-product-compliance
Lightning Source LLC
LaVergne TN
LVHW091134080826
845145LV00008B/2143
* 9 7 8 0 9 7 9 2 9 9 3 9 1 *